Praise for
ALL SYSTEMS GO

All Systems Go is well researched and practical and will prove helpful in developing systems that make businesses run more efficiently and productively. Zenovia has successfully simplified what often intimidates many businesses and entrepreneurs—systems! - **James R. Womack, M.H.S.A., Th.M.**

Systems could be one of the most misunderstood and underutilized tools inside organizations. Many times the CEO or entrepreneur is too wrapped up in expanding or strategizing to truly examine the state of their systems. Whether businesses realize it or not, they have systems, but for the majority of businesses, their systems are unintentional and therefore healthy. This is where Zenovia Andrews and her MAXOUT mentality come into play.

I personally know and consider it an honor to call Zenovia a friend. This relationship has allowed me to get to know her heart and passion for life and helping business owners. Also, I am a "systems guy." I believe in and fully understand the value of systems in healthy organizations. While there are plenty of business books out there, very few will match her understanding, passion for, and strategic plan to help you develop systems for your business. If you want to improve or transform your business or get the proper structure for a new venture, I highly recommend *All Systems Go* as a great place to get started. Let Zenovia and her wisdom help you "MAXOUT" your life and business! - **Ben Lile**s

ALL
SYSTEMS
GO

SURELY THERE IS A MORE CONSISTENT WAY TO DO THIS

ZENOVIA ANDREWS
FOREWORD BY LISA NICHOLS

This book is dedicated to:

My two amazing children: **Anovia and Anthony Jr.**
I pray that one day this book might serve as a road map
for success as you embrace your own journey in life

ACKNOWLEDGMENTS

To *Anthony* (my loving husband) – thanks for your constant love and patience. Your belief in me allows me to chase after my dreams. I can't imagine sharing this journey with anyone but you!

To the *MaxOUT Team* – for your tireless hours on this project to make this material available to everyone across this great world.

To the *entrepreneurs all across America* who have had the courage to build their dreams from scratch and do it unapologetically. You embracing the MaxOUT Methodology of creating business systems have provided you with wealth and happiness.

CONTENTS

FOREWORD

Zenovia has hit the ball out of the stadium with *All Systems Go*! The formula's insight and techniques that she provides are nothing short of brilliant. As a young aspiring business owner, what I knew how to do really well was to inspire people from the stage to the next level of their greatness. I admittedly was not strong in the development of the infrastructure and systems in my business. I spent a great deal of time, energy, and money making unnecessary mistakes and living with unnecessary stress. Once I incorporated effective systems into my business and learned the steps that Zenovia is teaching you in *All Systems Go*, my business began to morph into something barely recognizable. My revenue grew over 258% the first year that I incorporated these masterful systems. My productivity shot through the ceiling, and my stress level dissipated when I became aware of the ME myth that Zenovia brilliantly describes and provide techniques to manage early in her book. Her level of detail and clarity sets you up to win big time.

Every business owner needs a mentor, good books to learn from, and the heart of a lion to be successful. Well, if your reading this book, then you have found the right mentor in Zenovia and the perfect book to learn from, and I would be willing to bet that you have a great roar.

Zenovia is on track to be one of the most sought after speakers in the industry based on her powerful message and the results that she facilitates in her students. I am happy that you have access to her brilliance right now.

Grab your highlighter and notepad, get super comfortable, and begin to watch your breathtaking future unfold as you read, digest, and implement this book.

Lisa Nichols
(My Business Mentor)

INTRODUCTION

THE GOAL OF BUSINESS

Running a business of any size can become all-encompassing—and attaining success with that business can and will become the center of your world.

In the past, "business success" has always been the driving force for any company, though it has been tragically portrayed as a vague point in time when all of your hard work and sacrifice is validated. This is rarely the case!

Terminology like this has spawned a generation of people that are driven to succeed but have no clear direction on how to do it. I believe that many business owners, professionals, and CEOs have forgotten the main goal of business.

Contrary to popular belief, a business is not simply a money-making vessel. What you put in is not always what you get out. In fact, there are some very tough realities that need to be revisited if you are ever truly going to find success for your business.

We all have our own special ways of making things work. Our personal "magic" is what keeps the cogs turning and your business earning! But surely there must be a better way? There must be a way to build a successful business without having to be there monitoring it 24/7. Otherwise your business is no better than an incapable child.

- Do you never have time to implement the strategies that will really make your business lift off the ground?
- Does your business suffer when you are not around?
- Do you struggle to nurture the fundamental pillars of business, including customer relationships, growth, profit, and efficiency?

I designed The MAXOut Framework to correct many of the most restrictive practices that are in place in the business world today that are keeping your business from its true potential. By teaching you how to systematize your business, you will transform an inconsistent earner into a powerful, self-running system that earns for you every day.

This exceptional framework will help you create effective business systems that will eliminate waste, inefficiency, and frustration while dramatically improving your customer loyalty, profitability, and growth. Your business IS meant to earn for you all the time—just not in the ways we were all taught by our parents.

Systems are easy to implement and easy to replicate. When you learn how to apply a solid framework to your business, that is when that authentic "business success" will start rolling forward. In one year you can correct the bad practices that have left you overworked, exhausted, and looking for answers.

WORKING WITH
LIFE SYSTEMS

"Everything must be made as simple as possible. But not simpler."

ALBERT EINSTEIN

I always like to compare the business world to real life because they both function best when one is influenced by the other. Your business can learn a lot about systems simply by observing the way the natural world works.

Everything in nature strikes a perfect, almost incomprehensible balance, like it is part of a great design, or framework, of its own. Compare this to your business right now, and I bet the term "balance" has nothing to do with the way you are running it.

What Are Systems?

A system can be defined as a set of detailed methods, routines, and procedures that are created to carry out a specific action or duty or to correct a lingering problem. Systems are made up of structures or frameworks that contribute to the planning and implementation process.

A number of different elements will make up these systems, and—when maintained—they will ensure that the "activity" or desired "result" is consistent and dependable. In nature there are systems everywhere—flawless, highly functional systems that guarantee certain species are able to thrive even under the most dire circumstances.

Bears, for example, spend all summer eating as much as they can so that by the time winter comes around, they can hibernate. It is a survival strategy that has ensured the existence of bears for centuries even though winters are getting colder and food is getting scarcer.

Sometimes a simple system can guarantee the survival of your business during those lean, cold months. Systems can also be put in place to combat lean months instead of escaping them. Systems can be used for any purpose, to any end.

It makes you wonder why all businesses are not implementing better systems all the time! Not only do they streamline your business processes but they give you an active system of feedback or measurement so that you can constantly improve that system.

You may be thinking—but I have systems! There is a big difference between a system and a process. Processes are those little "systems" you create but never verify. They consume time and money and can create excess without you ever fully understanding them.

It is sad and ironic that business owners that do not have the time to systemize their businesses are the ones that need to the most. That is why I have written this book: to allow you to transition from an unstructured system to something much, much better!

Our World of Systems

If you want to fully understand the importance of systems, just take a look at the modern human world today. There are systems of government and political systems—there is even a system that is used to create the geographical appearance of a new developing area. Roads, buildings, and traffic are all parts of a system.

Now you have to ask yourself why. Why so many systems? Simply because systems are the only way something will work, all the time. Another way of saying this is that systems guarantee a certain outcome.

Imagine the power of this concept in your business! Imagine being able to depend on the income or growth of your company. It would change your life. We are all born with unique ideas and the potential to become system innovators—but first you need to have a system!

Now imagine if the world operated like your business and there were not any systems to rely on. There would be war, with power struggles everywhere. No one would have time to focus on service delivery or upkeep because everyone would be preoccupied with the huge amount of work they had to do and fighting for survival.

This is exactly what happens to a business that does not use systems. Resources are misappropriated, human capital devalues—and suddenly everyone becomes overworked, yet the business does not grow or earn any extra income. What cannot be measured cannot be improved, as they say.

The modern world has many systems that keep things in order for us. We know we can go somewhere to get gas or electricity and that these will not run out anytime soon. Not only does the country benefit but the people do as well.

In your business, when there is an absence of balance, it is you and your employees that suffer. Instead of focusing on the core problems, the individuals that make up the business have to look for ways to increase their workload just to keep going. In these lean economic times, this spells disaster or worse—failure.

Systems exist as vital structures that can be improved upon over time. When there is no system, there is no improvement—and this has been your fundamental downfall. These days, without consistent improvement, you might as well close your doors.

The Business of Systems

Zooming in a little closer, we can see how the largest and most successful businesses in the world focus on their systems. Without these set systems, franchise models would not exist. What greater example of a business that uses modern systems than to sneak a peek into the inner workings of a fast food giant like Subway?

Like many systemized businesses, Subway relies on fast, efficient operations and practices conducted by any one of their several thousand staff members to execute down to the letter. You see, a good system can be repeated and used by anyone. A great system is so easy that it produces the exact same result every time.

For the Subway business model to work, each delicious sub needs to be made the exact same way—because customers expect that same taste. If a customer walks in to any one of their many stores nationwide and gets something different, there will be trouble.

Good systems are good business, plain and simple. For Subway, a system might begin at the bread recipe stage. They bake their own bread using a carefully designed system that optimizes their time and projected sales for the day.

Then the bread is added to their service system, and customers enter the store and order to complete the process. A friendly staff member creates the perfect sub for you, and off you go—happy with your Subway sandwich.

There are many points in this process that could result in problems, but over a period of trial and error, testing, and reassessment, the ideal system has been realized. Can you imagine if this system did not exist? Bread would be baked incorrectly, it would be ready late, customers would not receive the same orders, and the company would break down.

Likewise, if there were no business systems in place to market Subway's tasty sandwiches, the brand would not be as popular. Specials would not be seen by customers, and entire marketing campaigns would fall to pieces.

Systematizing your business is like preparing it for inevitable success. Whatever your niche, whatever your business—you will benefit from the powerful inclusion of simple systems into your business model and culture.

Think about your business as it stands right now. Is there room for improvement? Are you already eager to begin creating systems that will take your business to the next level in your niche?

Your Life in Systems

You have seen how the world operates using systems and how some of the most successful businesses in the world use systems for success. But there is another way we use systems that is counterproductive to this imminent change.

People tend to systemize their lives. We have to if we are going to get through the sheer amount of work we have to do each and every day. A single business owner can go to work for an entire week, spend 10 hours there each day, and STILL not get anything done.

This is because you are building systems around your life instead of around your business! Think about your average day: You get up at the same time, and you shower and brush your teeth in the same way. You make breakfast; it is usually the same thing. You drive to work and conduct your "morning routine," right?

Then work begins. Even though you do not realize it, you have systematized your life in a way that best suits you. For business owners, this leads to one thing—being overworked! You will sacrifice your personal life in order to succeed at business because this is what you believe needs to happen in order to become successful.

Well, I am here to tell you that it is simply not true. Stop trying to fit your life into a business context! Life is about more than business, and when you allow work to consume it, no one benefits at the end of the day.

Would it not be better to systematize your business so that it functions properly without you? Of course it would! You need to stop trying to make a square peg fit into a round hole! That means you have to stop relying on the automatic processes that make up your day and start creating systems that optimize your day.

Systems are a natural part of life and an incredibly powerful tool in business. I do not know why so many people insist that these systems are not needed when they clearly are. If you cannot measure or test any part of your business operations, then you are not doing enough FOR your business.

In a way, you are being selfish and making your business all about you. But businesses do not have instincts, and your employees will not follow your vision if there are no systems in place to ensure it. They will follow their own systematized lives, which usually results in "as little work as possible."

Becoming a Systems Thinker

So systems are everywhere, except in your business! That is why you need to reshape yourself into a business systems thinker. When you begin to see your business through the eyes of a systems creator, everything changes.

You have a new business goal. Instead of trying to force increased profits, focus on becoming a results-orientated company. Take that next logical leap and start to see each and every function as something that can be streamlined for success.

- Change your mindset about your business. It cannot run based on the personal decisions of your employees; they need guidance through systems.

- Off the top of your head, pick a time-consuming process that you conduct every day. Focus on seeing where you can cut time, improve procedures, and make the function work for you.

- Start to understand how systems work and how actions taken can easily impact results over time.

- Become a "big picture" thinker to see how each individual system component works together to create one large, systematized machine that works smoothly.

- Understand that nothing stands still and that everything changes over time. You must be willing to update your systems constantly for them to work.

- Focus on system interdependencies, or who needs to work together to create successful outcomes in your new systematized business.

- Consider different models, from all perspectives, and the short- or long-term consequences that change will have on your company.

Becoming a systems thinker will help you transition from an internal role of authority to an external role of authority. Think of it like this—when you are overwhelmed with work, you are blind to the other problems happening in your company.

When you are not working and are instead focused on your business, that is when you will be able to approach systematization holistically for the good of your company and everyone in it. Eventually you will be so good at creating and implementing new systems that you will be able to create new businesses founded on the same established systems.

The first step to becoming a systems thinker is to cast off your current identity as a "hard worker" and reframe how you see yourself in the context of your business.

The ME Investment Myth

Work hard at school, and get a degree. Get a job; maybe open your own company one day. This is the advice we were all given not too long ago. But there is a myth going around that is at least twenty years old.

I call it the ME Investment myth. Tell anyone around you that you are starting a new business, and you will get the same outdated advice: "You better be ready to work hard, long hours," and "Owning a business takes up nearly all of your time."

As a result, people prepare themselves for a completely unbalanced business experience. Instead of preparing your business for battle, you prepare yourself for battle—and it is the worst possible thing you can do in modern business today.

You should not invest yourself in the daily running of your business! It is a total myth that YOU are expected to operate and run the business you conceptualized. I see it all the time: 75-year-old people that cannot retire because all they invested in their businesses was themselves. They became the engine behind the business.

What should happen is that systems become the engine behind your business. When they do not do this, your business will crumble if you do not pitch up for work. Transitioning from "doing" to "leading" is a tough step but an essential one.

Delegating work is pointless when you are a "doer" because the work will never be done as well as you could do it and the quality drops. This is especially true in service-based businesses. Now, if you work on a system instead, there is every chance that you will achieve the same quality levels based on attempts that you have measured.

- This is why you need to avoid the ME Investment Myth and instead embrace your new future as a leader—a systems thinker.

If you want your business as a whole to grow, you need to lead it to growth. You will never be able to do that while bogged down in paperwork and the "little" things. Growing really does mean learning to work ON your business and not IN your business.

In a quote on Forbes, Nina Vaca, owner of Pinnacle, said, *"Some business owners spend so much time working on their weaknesses and trying to be everything but the problem is that company will only grow to the limits of the talents of that individual. You want it to grow to the talents of the entire team. It takes a group to move an organization forward. Once owners understand that, they are well on their way to success."*

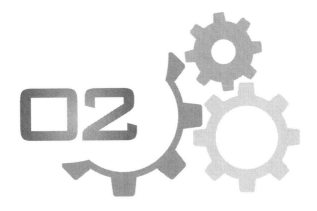

THE MAXOUT METHODOLOGY

"Sometimes when you innovate, you make mistakes. It is best to admit them quickly, and get on with improving your other innovations."

STEVE JOBS

Amidst the chaos of your average business day, the thought crosses your mind—surely there is a better way to do this. It was this single thought that led me to develop the MAXOut Methodology for my clients and friends.

It is not enough to want to create systems in business; you need to know HOW so that you do not have to make a million and five mistakes first. Using a framework like the one I have created here will guide you towards systematic success in no time.

What Is the MAXOUT Methodology?

The world is full of jargon, and as a business coach, I am acutely aware of how damaging that jargon can be. I have seen people take the systems fix to heart only to undergo serious problems during implementation.

No business change is ever easy, and there will always be a need for a smooth transition to something new. The MAXOut methodology does this in the easiest way possible. Each letter stands for a part of the system that you will need to work through.

- **M** stands for Measurable Actions.
- **A** stands for Automated Systems.
- **X** stands for X-treme Distancing.
- **O** stands for Operations Management.
- **U** stands for Understanding Profitability.
- **T** stands for Thinking Ahead.

As you can see, the system is made up of actionable steps that you can take in order to progress to a point where you have your own systematized business. This methodology will turn a business that relies on YOUR hard work into a self-running system that guarantees you results day after day.

It is designed to multiply your profit potential by turning your business into an entity that focuses on the one thing we all need most as business people—money! I am talking about consistent growth, trimming the fat, improving every last operation in your company, AND freeing your time so that you can finally become the captain of your ship.

Until now you have been in the boiler room, shoveling coal into the fire. But as I have explained, when you shovel coal, you cannot see where the ship is going. Expect this incredible methodology to solve several key concerns:

- How to create your own customized formula for greater profitability
- How to use a one-year action plan to improve customer loyalty and attraction
- How to grow and maintain a business that never stands still

How It Prepares You for Success

In a nutshell, the MAXOut Methodology will teach you how to systematically create the best operations, production, and marketing methods in the world that will keep your business growing and gathering profit—like a snowball rolling down a mountainside!

I want to take this opportunity to identify a few people that could be reading this book right now and wondering—but is this for me? The truth is that this system is for everyone.

- Business owners, small and large
- Executives
- Companies that find their systems stagnating
- Corporations
- Project Managers
- CEO or CFOs
- Entrepreneurs

Bottom line—this methodology works on a formula that does not fail. Let me explain why when you make the switch, big things will happen for your company.

Example 1: Right now you own a business. It may be doing well; it may not be. Somehow you have figured out that your business is not growing or expanding fast enough. Perhaps it is growing but in directions you refuse to acknowledge. You work hard—I mean really hard—but nothing seems to change.

FORMULA: Inconsistent behavior = inconsistent results

Example 2: Right now you own a business, and it is expanding at a rapid pace. You are no longer involved in the daily operations but instead focus on measurable metrics that can be used for quality decision-making. Your entire business from start to finish is documented and runs on the MAXOut methodology of systematizing your income.

FORMULA: Systematic behavior = predictable results!

What you want is to move from inconsistent behavior to systematic behavior. You want to transition from inconsistent results to predictable ones. The MAXOut methodology prepares you for success by helping you through this difficult transition.

You will not only revamp the way you do business but the way you think about business. In many ways, this may be one of the greatest leaps you make in your career. Using a combination of tried and tested strategies, I will take you from zero to hero in one short year. All strategies take time, but the results will come quickly.

If you are serious about rebuilding your business—or perhaps starting a new business with these principles—then the MAXOut methodology is the exact framework that will help you get there. These days, only the strong survive in business. And the strongest always have a customized system that moves all the right cogs at the right time.

The Benefits of a Solid Framework

A solid framework like the MAXOut methodology strips away the jargon and empowers you to create a custom plan that is unique to your business. Usually this would cost a fortune if you hired a business consultant to do it. So let's talk business. How exactly can this framework help you?

- Enjoy improved and consistent performance. The best businesses are performance-based down to the micro-level. You will experience improvements across the board, in every area, when you begin to systematize with MAXOut.

- Innovation becomes part of your business culture. This means that you will be able to come up with and implement new ideas whenever they strike.

- With a quality framework, you will be able to integrate new employees into your business culture in no time. They will be working at full capacity much faster than in an unstructured environment.

- This framework will allow you to step back, have more time off, be more innovative, and spend more time on higher-value activities so that your business takes off.

- Even one high-functioning system increases the equity value of your business. With MAXOut, systematizing your entire business will result in it gaining a lot of additional equity value.

- The right systems allow you to break individual processes down to their micro-parts. Instead of doing a lot to no effect, you will be able to improve performance in exact locations— where your business needs it the most.

- Even a small street vendor can achieve perfection and world-class performance when they systematize and measure their new activities. Finally, you will have a system of measurement that will tell you if what you are doing works.

- All of your systems will fit together like cogs in a well-oiled machine. This in turn will result in improved customer relationships and loyalty, greater profits, better operations, and a leaning towards innovation and invention.

- Move from a people-dependent business to a process-dependent business that can run independently of your input with your current staff or with new staff. The business by itself works; the people do not make the business.

As you can see, the MAXOut methodology is one framework that is poised to help you sort out those irritating problems that every business runs into. I am talking about weak sales, poor cash flow, terrible customer service, and low income. Who wants to struggle every day just to make sure all of the employees are paid? Not you!

Working with All Crucial Business Elements

Have you ever heard the old adage "pay yourself first"? It is one that many people know about and few can practice. Business owners dock their own paychecks first when things go wrong. CEOs of larger companies put in extra hours so that they do not have to fire additional staff members.

When a business functions on its own, all crucial business elements are covered. Think of it like this: Your goal is to bake a delicious cake. You spend all of your time focusing on the cake because you believe that is how it will sell. Unfortunately, you forget about the other elements—cake decorations to make it look good and a sales promotion to tell people about it.

Suddenly your cake does not sell, even though it may be the finest in the world. All businesses are made up of front-end and back-end operations. From money concerns to staffing, service delivery, customer relationship management, and sales, I will almost bet that there is not an even balance in the way that you develop these key areas.

The MAXOut methodology systematizes ALL parts of your business so that the business—from start to finish—works flawlessly. There will never be a product you cannot sell. There will never be a low quality product. You will have the right people, and you will have the right approach to customers—because you covered all the bases.

The MAXOut methodology covers all of these bases and more. It is completely scalable and encourages a continuous cycle process so that re-evaluation and improvement become central to your business culture. Let's take another look at what this methodology offers you.

- *Measurable Actions:* Learn how measuring processes in your business is the most direct route to business growth.

- *Automated Systems:* Learn how to establish various automated systems to free up your time so that you can focus on "big picture" strategy.

- *X-treme Distancing:* Learn how to transition from working in your business to working on your business—for maximum returns.

- *Operations Management:* Learn how to focus on the people in your business and to create a climate of results-driven performance.

- *Understanding Profitability:* Learn about the golden rules of finance and how to systematize your income and cash flow for exponential growth.

- *Thinking Ahead:* Learn to refocus your mind on progressing your business to the next level by being a business leader, not a business worker.

Using System Cycles for Business Success

Systematizing your business means allowing it to operate in a certain way. But it also means tracking, analyzing, and restructuring these operations in a way that best suits the business. Using the MAXOut methodology, you will do this using system cycles for success.

The plan is split into three parts:

1. System Success Cycles
2. System Involvement Cycles
3. System Money Cycles

Each of these cycles will ensure that you periodically improve on the changes that you make for your business. Put simply—at the end of every chapter, you will have the opportunity to work out your very own "cycle" based on the information that I provide.

System cycles can be expanded or limited based on what your business is all about. They will contain several strategies that will help you fully systematize your company. A few examples might be:

- In the System Measurement Cycle, you will find several elements that will help you greatly improve the manner in which you measure key performance indicators in your business. From measuring your financial strategies to measuring your customer-related systems, these are all concerns that you will need to work on as you read this book.

- At the very end of every cycle is a step toward the beginning of a new cycle—so the process of re-evaluation never ends. I have specifically done this because I believe that it is pointless systematizing your business only to allow those systems to become out-dated and detrimental to the health and growth of your company.

- First and foremost, all cycles should have you testing and implementing new things. Your new role in your business will involve deciding how best to stay abreast of evolving processes. In every niche, there are new technologies, new processes, and more efficient ways to get from A to Z with every passing year.

By splitting the MAXOut methodology into these three parts, you will end up with over 30 different strategies that lead into a quality success cycle process. I would suggest that you use this book first to orientate yourself with systematization and to help restructure your business in a practical sense—using the blueprint areas and success cycles.

Your MAXOut Success Blueprint

If I am going to be honest, I have never found much use for a purely informational business book. They are great to get you excited for what it is you have to do, but if they do not explain how to get things done, they have little value.

That is why at the end of each chapter I include a blueprint outline. In these sections, I will ask you some very important questions that will help you put together a "master" systematization blueprint for your company.

This is what I call the MAXOut Success Blueprint. By the time you get to the final chapter, you will have everything you need to begin the systematization process. Remember, if you think of any other areas that can be improved, add them in!

No business book can tell every individual owner how to run their business. There are too many variable factors involved. That is why I want you to think of the MAXOut methodology as your personal route to systematization success.

- Incorrectly creating systems in your business can lead to income loss, employee dissatisfaction, and even more work loaded on people that are barely doing the work they already have.

Think of this book as a navigation tool, pointing true north for your business. It will take any unstable, struggling business and transform it into a stable, reliably profitable one. That is the goal you are working towards here. No more financial worry; no more working 16-hour days. Business is only worthwhile when you focus on the right things.

Too many people have looked inward and built business around their own skills and talents. Too many CEOs have maintained out-dated practices that are devaluing their own business presence in the modern age. It is time to step out from behind the blinkers to sort out the problems that you have been having.

Your MAXOut Success Blueprint will be the document that takes you all the way to the top. Use it as your master planning document; a place where you can create new processes, implement ideas, test, discover, and measure.

This is your business, and it is time that you began to run it properly. No one wants to have to sacrifice years of their life to a business that does not reward them as planned. "Pay yourself first" will only start to make sense once you have enough time to use that brain of yours in the appropriate ways.

SYSTEM SUCCESS CYCLES

MEASURABLE ACTIONS

"Measurement is the first step that leads to control and eventually to improvement. If you can't measure something, you can't understand it. If you can't understand it, you can't control it. If you can't control it, you can't improve it."

H. JAMES HARRINGTON

Taking action is only the first step along your path to systematizing your business. In this first section of your System Success Cycle, I am going to speak about the processes in your business and what steps you are taking to evaluate their efficiency in your company.

You probably use dozens of processes in your business every single day. From how you answer the phone, to ordering stock, to dealing with a customer via email—these all add up to create the company that you have right now.

The Value of Every Process

I do not have to tell you that every process in your business is valuable. If there is a link missing in the chain, the business is not going to move forward. Remember, the MAXOut methodology is a holistic approach to business systematization and success.

As you putter along in your normal business day, you actually fix certain processes if there is a glaring error. For example, if a customer was not satisfied with your service and you botched the response, you will make a note to improve on that the next time.

Business processes can be both formal and informal depending on where their focus lies. Formal processes are what you want to work on at this stage. These processes are well-documented, and they detail step-by-step procedures on how to get things done correctly.

- Do you have documentation for your current formal processes?
- If not, start thinking about how formal outlines would improve your business.

I am a firm believer in documentation. If someone acts in your business (takes action), then there needs to be a "how" to match with that action. Little things like invoice submissions can even be systematized if you find the right tool and establish your documentation.

This is why I want you to map all the processes you can think of right now.

- Create flowcharts on how you conduct each process.
- Make a note of what the outcome usually is for each process.
- Ask yourself, can these outcomes be improved?
- Attempt to formulate a theory on how your processes can be improved.

The "Measure It" Rule

Measuring faulty business processes begins with identification and mapping. Once you have done that, you can start your very first set of tests. There is a rule that must be followed in the MAXOut methodology, and that is "everything must be measured."

- Based on your initial process assessment, create a brief report.

- Based on your idea for improvement, establish testing parameters.
- Use some kind of software to assist you.
- Set a testing time period, and capture your results.
- Document the results of your tests.

I suggest tiering your measurements in a way that best reflects your goals for your business. For example, if customers are your top priority, then profit, operations, and the rest will be arranged in order of importance below that.

There are a million ways to test something, but you will have to choose the method that is right for you. Measurement can be savagely simple or extremely complex. An example of measuring something in a simple manner includes:

- *Assessment:* What is the current state of management? What are the strengths and weaknesses?
- *Mapping:* This involves identifying elements or areas that need improvement, trimming, or development.
- *Analysis and Selection:* Based on the goals that you have set for this feature (management), which scenarios would improve X, Y, or Z? Choose one.
- *Development and Implementation:* Create documentation detailing how the management process will change and what the new procedures to follow are. Implement them and enforce their implementation.
- *Tracking and Measuring:* Finally, track the progress of your new procedure. After the test period is over, measure the effectiveness of the process and revise.

Measuring all of your processes is a long and difficult task in the beginning. But I did warn you that this is going to take about a year to get right! The purpose of this chapter is let you know what you will have to pay attention to in order to get your systems off the ground.

Not only will you be documenting and mapping every process but you will also be measuring each process. It is tempting to just accept that an old process is fine, but keep in mind that this defeats the whole point. If you do not integrate all facets of your business into the MAXOut methodology, then some parts will excel and others will cause problems.

Creating System Benchmarks

At the very beginning of your systematization process, you will need to establish your process benchmarks so that you can accurately assess each core procedure. This means knowing how to create a benchmark plan.

A benchmark can be defined as a point of reference from which measurements can be made. If you do not know where you have come from, how will you know where you are going? These are the standards that you need to improve on.

PLAN → COLLECT → ANALYZE → ADAPT

The Planning Phase

Begin by creating a team of people that will help you benchmark your business processes. Then identify, analyze, and document each and every process. Identify critical success factors and critical problem areas.

Once this is done, you can set your benchmarking scope and create a purpose statement. Create a data collection plan, and determine how it will be used. Finally, identify how the improvements will be accomplished.

The Collection Phase

During the collection phase, you will be conducting secondary research on your processes. Evaluate your results, and start looking at data collection tools. Conduct a detailed investigation into the data that you are analyzing , and draw insights from it.

The Analysis Phase

In the analysis phase, you will need to compare your current or existing performance data to your new process idea. Identify any gaps or operational best practices, and cite them in your documentation. Formulate a strategy to make the new process seamless. Develop a solid implementation plan.

The Adapting Phase

In the adaptation phase, you will implement your new and improved process! Then you will monitor and report on the progress for the entire time that you have outlined. Document this study and take the results seriously. Plan for continuous improvement by setting new, measurable goals at the end of each benchmarking phase.

- Focus on process mapping.
- Focus on performance measurements.
- Detail project management capabilities.
- Outline any questions, observations, or legal or ethical problems.

Each process must have identifiable benchmarks so that you can move forward with your measurement process. All of these measurements begin somewhere, and benchmarking gives you an excellent place to begin.

Establishing Rules and Measurement Processes

There are many different ways to measure a single process. You will have to set specific measurement processes and rules before you begin testing and measuring your new processes. That means identifying how to measure your processes correctly.

Many performance measures can be part of these six areas. Depending on your mission and goals, these can change.

- *Effectiveness* – Is the process doing the right things?
- *Quality* – Does the process meet the requirements and expectations?
- *Efficiency* – Is the process being done correctly?
- *Safety* – Does the process contribute to the safety of the employees and customers?
- *Timeliness* – Is the process done well in the planned out time?
- *Productivity* – What value does the process add to the business in relation to labor, capital, time, and cost-efficiency?

It is important to establish these units of measurement so that you can control, self-assess, improve, and manage all of the processes that enter your measurement cycles. As a general rule, you should only measure what is most important. You can identify what is important because it impacts your business—improving it or making it worse.

Be very careful that you document your measurement processes especially well as they will act in conjunction with whatever tools you decide to use for assistance. At this stage, you will sort out how you are going to measure each process and establish the criteria for later use.

- Use the benchmarks as a starting point.
- Establish the process measurements that need to be performed on each process.

Couple this with tools (in the blueprint section):

- Business process monitoring
- Business system performance monitoring
- Simulating and optimizing each process

Then Use This Formula as a Measurement Tool:

Valuable process + benchmarking + measurement criteria = a framework for transforming any existing process into a process that is ready to be systematized.

It is very important that you are directly involved in this process as part of your new role. If there was ever something to work hard on, it is this. Discovering what your key performance indicators are is not easy and neither is establishing a system for measuring processes in a specific niche. If you need to expand on this, do so. Knowledge is power!

Setting Goals and System Deployment

You need to set goals for each process that you measure so that when you do deploy a system of measurement for a particular process, it works well. I suggest a dashboard of some kind that visually displays your measurement system for insight analysis.

- Set a solid batch of tiered goals for every process.
- Establish your measurement system, and make sure that your metrics are correct.
- Educate your staff on how to use the new system of measurement.
- Make sure that there is ownership and accountability with this process.

- Each metric should have a group of goals that are in line with your business strategy.
- Try to close performance gaps by educating your staff about this new system.
- Human behavior needs to change from the beginning if this is going to work.
- Roll out your measurement system with tight control and management rules.

Depending on the size of your business, you will want to create an integrated deployment plan so that you can release the measurement system at a time when all of your employees are eager to see it succeed. A communication strategy would be appropriate here.

With any new system deployment, you will be required to monitor these measurement steps thoroughly. Once the benchmarks and units of measurement have been established and the new system deployed, it comes down to the people using the system.

I suggest that you roll out your measurement system and assign it to key people so that control and management is spread across multiple departments if your business has more than 50 people in it. Expect the measurement system development process to take anywhere between one and four months to complete.

The goal of this entire process is to establish where your key performance indicators lie. These KPIs will be the basis of every area that you are going to test. For example, customer relationship management may include customer service, call center processes, systems integration, online customer experience, and feedback.

In every area that is detailed, the number of parts makes up the whole (customer relationship management), which should be scored and rated so that it can be re-assessed in a few months' time. You should never stop creating, assessing, and deploying systems at any time. If you do, then you have allowed your business to become stagnant.

Blueprint 1: The System Measurement Cycle

The first blueprint needs to address how you will measure your various operations once you have them established and working.

Establish the Areas in Your Business That Promote Success

- Profit
- Customers
- Employees
- Operations
- Growth

There are five KPIs (key performance indicators) that will let you know if your business is improving from the changes that you have made. You will learn about these later on. For now, how do you plan on measuring the impact of your various business systems?

Once You Have Identified the Areas, Formulate Your Measurement Strategy

- Do you have a tool to measure each strategy within these KPIs?
- Which tools will you use?
- Who will be using these tools?
- When will you use these tools?
- Identify which metrics are most important from each section.

I suggest searching online for common methods of measurement that are used in your niche. Sometimes they can be simple programs; other times you may have to specifically purchase software in order to keep track of different business segments.

Technology is essential when building quality business measurement systems. They will help you automatically track and interpret how each strategy is doing over time.

The average test period for new business operations or methods are broken into one-, two-, and three-month increments. Any measurement cycle should run for three months as a short-term test and six months as a long-term test.

Collect as much information about these various tools as you can. Apply for test trials if you have to. When you reach a later chapter, we will go into more detail about how to use these details in a success cycle. Apply this cycle to any new KPI that you want to measure in order to keep it improving over short and long time periods.

AUTOMATED SYSTEMS

"The first rule of any technology used in a business is that automation applied to an efficient operation will magnify the efficiency. The second is that automation applied to an inefficient operation will magnify the inefficiency."

BILL GATES

The second part of your success cycle focuses on automating systems that matter to your business. Right now there are dozens of systems that can be drastically improved if only you knew how to automate them!

For some inexplicable reason, automation has had some bad press over the last few years, but there is nothing wrong with making your business more efficient by automating systems that you and your employees do not need to deal with on a daily basis!

The Power of Systematic Automation

Systematically automating your business is probably one of the best things you can do to improve all processes on multiple levels. It does not matter what you do only that you optimize every aspect of what you do.

A very big part of this is discovering the areas in your business that can be improved (and even perfected) without any human interference at all. There is real power in systematic automation. Let me paint you a picture so that you understand what I mean.

For the average small business, invoicing is always a long and time-consuming process. Most of the time there is zero system in place to create, send, or check on the invoices that have been sent to clients. By implementing a new software system, this small business can completely streamline their invoicing processes.

This may not mean much when you think about it at first, but there are far reaching consequences. First of all, you no longer have to think about who has or has not been invoiced or who has and has not paid. It is all there, which means no more forgotten, late, or unpaid bills. There are even reminders that are automatically sent to the customer.

Not only does the small business owner save time creating invoices at the click of a button, but financial management, process execution, and customer relationships are all improved. By automating the invoicing process, the business improves, grows, and gives the owner more money sooner and more time to work on what matters.

That is just one small automated component that can rapidly and significantly improve the way your business operates. Large, medium, and small companies need to identify areas where automation will help their business operate more efficiently. Then they need to implement automated systems that work so that they do not have to.

Automating Customer Loyalty

All businesses need to be concerned about the service that they provide to their customers. There are always 10 other businesses just like yours that will take your place if at any time your existing customers are not happy with your products, services, or business.

Automating customer loyalty has become a very popular way of guaranteeing that the "usual characters" walk through your doors. Repeat business needs to be one of your main priorities, specifically because the market is "buyer-centric" now.

The average consumer has so many choices that they do not

have to shop at your store, buy your products, or do business with you. All business owners need to find a method of adding value through a loyalty program that can be automated.

Your Main Goals for Automating Customer Loyalty

- Consolidate customer data by uniting it all under one software program. Your email lists, point of sale system lists, online order lists, and even website lists can be consolidated and leveraged for automated customer retention.
- Create a rewards or incentive system that answers the question—why will my target repeat customer choose to come back to my business? You can devise a points system or keep it simple by adding special discounts and coupons to your weekly email and SMS blasts.
- Use your customer loyalty incentives to attract new business and to connect with your existing communities online. If you run a competition, publish the media on your social platforms. Share an incredible coupon with exclusive members, and take photos for your Facebook and Pinterest pages.

Achieving Customer Loyalty Automation

As an entrepreneur, you will need to investigate the many automated systems that can help you realign and perfect the connections that you have with your customers. Try to solve these questions when dealing with new software:

- Does it connect my business to my ideal customer regularly without any constant maintenance or direct contact?
- Does it help me leverage my coupons, discounts, and deals to the right audience at the right time?

- Does it help you to better understand your customers' buying behavior by forming profiles and collecting valuable customer data?

- Does it help you predict future purchasing behavior based on data analyzed from past interactions with your brand?

Depending on your niche, you will be introduced to a number of various software programs that can improve the way you engage, connect, and add value to your customer interactions. A good automated customer loyalty program is exactly what you need to focus your customer relationship management practices on.

Automating Employee Satisfaction

In your business, everyone has a job to do, and it is their responsibility to do it well. As the entrepreneur or owner, however, it is your job to make sure that all of your resources—including your human resources—are functioning at their best.

When you take the time to automate many of the time-consuming processes that employees have to deal with on a daily basis, several things happen. Employees' time is put to better use, they feel valued and appreciated, and staff turnover remains low. When you have happy people working in your business, you have a happy business!

Your Main Goals for Automating Employee Satisfaction

- Spot the areas that can be automated without the direct help of your employee. If you have an office worker, for example, you can help them be efficient by automating many of their basic admin tasks, automating how they are paid, and even automating how stock is ordered. That way they are left to better deal with your customers.

- You will need to manage the change in your workplace. Automating systems can leave your employees feeling threatened, like you are going to automate them out of a job. Make it clear that you are only optimizing their jobs so that they can spend more time doing the important things.

- Automating things like payment and stock ordering keeps your employees happy. An employee that is paid on time, every time is secure in their work—a big hurdle for small businesses. Stock ordering can also be a source of contention, so when it is automated, internal work relationships improve and evolve.

How to Make Your Employees' Jobs Easier

To increase employee satisfaction, sit down with your employees and discuss how you can improve their daily productivity by automating parts of their job that can be streamlined in this way. When you make your employees' jobs easier, they can dedicate more of their energy to sales, helping customers, and growing your business.

Remember, you are not one of your employees—but we will get into this a little later in the book. For now you need to automate everything your employees do not need to be doing manually each and every day.

Research the kind of software programs that can help you solve these automation challenges. They often come individually, or in packs, to consolidate several areas of your business into one niche-automation package.

Automating Sales & Marketing

Sales and marketing is perhaps the most essential part of any business in this highly competitive niche marketplace. You need to realize that much of your marketing can be automated, which will result in stronger leads and increased sales.

Whether you own an online business or a corner store – the principle is the same. Being in the online space is something that you cannot ignore in this day and age. In fact, automating a large part of your sales and marketing will actually make sure that your company survives despite the influx of rampant, innovative competition from all over the globe.

Your Main Goals for Automating Sales & Marketing

- Marketing automation is a secret kept by many wealthy online marketers—and for good reason. It rapidly improves the buying potential of one customer, resulting in more sales, repeat visits, higher online conversions, and even word of mouth marketing. Done right, it can work for your business while your employees work in your business.

- There are dozens of software providers that can equip your business with the right marketing automation software. Anything from lead capture, drip campaigns, multichannel social media marketing and tracking, lead scoring, management, real time conversion events, and instant CRM integration is available to anyone that understands the value of automation.

- Keep a firm eye on email marketing, social marketing, marketing management, analytics, and sales insight to instantly and consistently improve your real world and online marketing processes. When you track your sales using high impact software, you can streamline how you market to your daily customers.

Taking the Business Pressure off Your Business

Lead generation and foot traffic are two of the most difficult things to maintain consistently in a business of any size. At any moment, your customer base can choose to shop elsewhere, or the bulk of your buying public can simply vanish. To prevent this, consistent marketing has become a normal monthly process.

However, you and your employees should not be worrying about the basic act of having people "visit" your store or use your services. Instead, you should be focusing on customer experience and fostering repeat business and good relationships. That is why marketing automation is key; it takes the pressure off your business to FIND business.

In one package, you can systematically source new business, convert old business, and sustain stronger, better buying relationships with your customer base. This leaves you with the elbow room you need to expand, grow, and improve other sales areas.

Automating Annual Growth

The case for niche area automation is strong, but what about automating your annual business growth? Remember, as a business owner and entrepreneur, your main job is to ensure that your business is progressing or growing consistently. Otherwise, what is the point? Now the question becomes—can I automate my business growth?

- Automating your customer loyalty program will help your business retain and convert the people that love to buy from your brand. While you are giving back in the form of discounts, competitions, and special deals, your customers will form a community around you that is always interested in what you have to sell or say.

- Automating your employee satisfaction improves the way your employees function and work together as a team in your company. When they are happy and motivated, they work harder for your success. This means that if you nurture your employees, your business will grow each year in terms of employee retention and potential.

- Automating your sales and marketing is an excellent way to keep people flowing through your business and people talking about your business. When your marketing improves, so do your business opportunities. Every year you should experience a significant increase in sales from the previous year.

Choosing the Right Automation Software

Automating your annual business growth boils down to being able to identify and select the right technology partners or software providers that can help you collect, track, and manage your various data streams and campaigns.

There are five stages of business growth: entrepreneurial, direction, delegation and functional management, co-ordination and monitoring, and collaboration and global organization. Depending on your needs and vision, knowing where your end goal lies is important to the growth process. Establish where you want to end up, and set a target from there.

Once you have discovered how large you want to grow, you can lay out a five-year plan, and then work out your projected annual growth plans based on the software that you select and begin using. It gets easier as you grow as long as automation is always a pillar you can rely on in your company.

Make sure that your automation software scales with your projected goals. If something does not work, then you must change your software and automated processes. Automation is only as good as the results it produces for you!

Blueprint 2: The System Automation Cycle

Let's take a moment to revisit the initial question about automation. Can this be done consistently without human interference? That is the question you will be applying to different areas of your business so that you can establish quality automated practices.

Identify Areas That Can Be Improved via Automation

- Individual projects
- Standing processes that require manual human input
- Data or admin work
- Sales and marketing targets
- Customer loyalty program development
- Employee management
- Stock control

These are some areas where you can greatly improve your business simply by integrating new automated processes into the foundation of your business culture. Do not be afraid of automation; it is there to make your life consistently easier.

After Identification, Source a Complete or Several Individual Software Packages

There are hundreds of different types of automated software. It is up to you as the business owner to research and discover the best software for people in your niche. Some software is specifically designed for a business area (marketing for example); others are tied to a niche-specific process like factory automation.

Depending on your financial investment and niche, you must choose the right pieces of software that will help you automate your business. This is how you close the system automation cycle and empower your business to run independently of excessive human input, which makes more time for the things that matter.

Implementation and Testing Phases

Automating manual processes in your business will give you strong tactical and strategic advantages over your competitors. In

20 years from now, it will be rare to find any business—small or large—that does not rely heavily on automation. Once you have chosen your software, you will need to implement and test it for a month.

If you can see significant improvements then, you are on the right track. Do monthly reports, and actively track how automation is improving your business. That way when something is not working as it should, you can identify it and make positive adjustments to your automation strategy.

The Areas to Focus On:

- Employee productivity
- Customer sales and repeat business
- Profit generation
- Business expansion
- Workflow
- Individual processes

SYSTEMS INVOLVEMENT CYCLES

X-TREME
DISTANCING

"Growing means learning to work on your business, not in it."

GERI STENGEL, FORBES

By far the most common entrepreneurial mistake is to be too emotionally invested in your business. In this section of the MAXOut Framework, you will learn why systematizing your involvement in your own business is essential to long-term success.

Entrepreneurs often cut corners and decide to directly run their businesses without much outside help. The result is that your business shuts down when you are not there. That is not a business model; that is a stress nightmare.

Your X-treme Business Dilemma

As an entrepreneur, you are used to "taking the heat" when it comes to your business. Long hours, hard work, and multitasking are just a few of the pitfalls of going into business by yourself. Suddenly you are the linchpin that holds your empire together; without you, everything would be a disaster.

You need to switch from a culture of "doing" to a culture of "leading." You cannot be a doer and a leader—you can only be one or the other. Doing everything in your business is not what a leader does. A leader delegates. They manage. They see where problems arise and then fix them. A leader does not do the books, the sales, the products, and everything else.

I am going to ask you one profound question—do you DO too much for your own business? Most of you that answer honestly will have to admit the truth—yes! There is always too much for you to deal with in the day-to-day running of your own company.

When you work IN your business and not ON your business, you fail to move forward. It is entirely impossible to be everything and everyone all at once and then still manage to make non-emotional, analytical decisions about business growth.

The reality is that when you are working hard—sorting out admin, staff, orders, or marketing—you are also NOT managing the success of your company. In this way, you not only spread yourself too thin, but you fail to be the leader your company needs for sustained, long-term growth and eventual success.

Real business freedom comes from the understanding that you cannot be responsible for the daily operations of your company. It is impossible. Imagine not only neglecting your primary role but dividing your skills, time, and resources so that no areas of your new business get any real attention. You would have to be a genius to make something like that work.

The Mechanical Rule of Distance

Distance is the one trait you need to adopt in order to correct this "over commitment" to your business. I call it the "mechanical rule of distance" because it is the easiest way to initially control and adjust your destructive business behavior.

- You cannot work FOR your own business.
- You cannot spend 16-hour days trying to make it work.
- You cannot burn yourself out trying to DO everything.
- You cannot keep your business open based on your effort alone.

The mechanical rule of distance tells us that your business should be able to run completely independently of your input.

If you want to take a week off, not only should you be able to do that, but you should have no worries about the solvency of your company while you are away. This is how you build a lasting business that will not shrivel up and die without you.

Start by understanding that you want to be an entrepreneur, not a workhorse. The two are often keenly misidentified. You will be told by other entrepreneurs that businesses are hard work, long hours, and tons of stress. Why? Surely if this was the way businesses begin, no large companies would exist at all!

From today, you have a new set of priorities. This is what they are:

- Be the overlord of your business finances.
- Be the visionary who plans and strategizes for your company.
- Focus on hiring, training, and developing the right people in your business.
- Involve everyone in the growth and success of your business.
- Hold everyone accountable for their actions.

In other words, you need to be the "big cheese" behind the work, not the work itself! It begins with you taking a seat and looking at how your business runs. By identifying how much you do and then transferring your key roles to other employees, you will free up your time to finally take the reins and drive your company towards success.

Real bosses only need to "pop in" to check on their businesses. Your new role as the head honcho will have you ensuring that OTHER people are doing their work correctly, on time, and according to the systems you have put in place. Never rely on an individual's ability; instead, use systems to teach them how you want them to behave in YOUR company.

Follow the mechanical rule of distance from now on by creating a plan—then changing over to being a boss and not a boss-employee. You cannot be your dream team; you have to build a dream team. No entrepreneur is an island. If you fail to follow this advice, you will end up 70 years old and unable to retire because your business relies on you for income.

Preparing Your Business for Winter Days

As an entrepreneur, I am sure that you are fully familiar with the constant lack of money that seems to permeate through your average week. No matter how many projects you take on or how many products you sell, there never seems to be enough money.

Despite what you have been told, this makes perfect sense. Bosses are in charge of imagining new ideas and creating strategies to put in place to generate larger sources of revenue. You have not been doing that, because you see your business through the eyes of an overworked, underpaid employee.

Being less involved in your day-to-day operations gives you ample time to assume your role as the visionary, planner, and drive behind your business. Preparing for "winter days," or slow sales days (or months), may be a reality for you. Imagine how much better at it you would be if you could focus all your time on solving the problem instead of working IN your business!

- A winter day is not a joke. You need contingency plans to ensure that your business can survive with no income for at least a year. Smaller businesses may have to focus on a few months to begin with. If your company cannot survive even a week of no income, you are mismanaging it!

- Hire and train staff that can plug "holes" during periods of income shortfall. You freaking out then spending thousands on flyers is not going to help you. However, hiring a marketing specialist (even temporarily) can give you the boost you need. You can also focus on training existing staff.

- Creating an atmosphere of balance, happiness, and flawless customer service will help you build a community around your brand. Being frazzled, dashing around in haste, and being irritable does not put out a good vibe for your company.

As the newly reinstated "boss," you will be charged with managing how your automated systems, business process systems, and employees handle times of scarcity. It is not your job, however, to shift into "marketing" gear under so much pressure. Financial pressure leads to poor decisions, and you can blow a lot of money in a desperate attempt to make some.

A winter day should not even register on your success radar, because you can create systems and contingencies and put plans in place to minimize or completely eliminate any strain, damage, or stress that comes from a slow month. Then when business calms down, your only goal will be to accelerate your existing marketing system plans.

The 5 Keys of Delegation

Your new mantra must now become "delegation first"! Because you will be stepping back to properly run and manage your company, you will need to learn how to adequately delegate all remaining tasks to other employees.

A prominent business mentor of mine always used to say, "Busy-ness is not business." That is why you have a lot of work to do on honing your delegation skills. There are five dominant keys to becoming a master of delegation.

#1. Understand that your team is made up of human beings. No one can work nonstop, so get your timing right. Know what each employee can handle, and never overwork them. People are at their best when they are consistently busy but not rushed or pressured.

#2. Focus on the strengths of your team. Delegation is not a dump and run tactic. You still need to know your employees and how they fit into your business puzzle. Play to their strengths, and give them responsibilities and authority.

#3. Focus on your own strengths, then plug the holes. It is great wanting to be the world's most amazing financial leader, but if that is just not you, then accept that. Instead, use your incredible marketing skills, for example, and hire an accountant to take care of the finances.

#4. Be the resource king or queen. Your employees are only as good as the resources they have. Make sure that they are equipped to always do the best work for you on a daily basis. Running out of stock, not having new software, and not shelling out for that desperately needed printer is NOT good delegation.

#5. Become the fire, ice, and motivation behind your team. When they need guidance, give it to them; when they need appreciation, offer it to them. Inspire, motivate, and lead by supporting your delegated decisions and following up on them often.

Without delegation, an entrepreneur can easily become like that famous story of the little Dutch boy that kept a dam from exploding by plugging a hole with his finger. You have been plugging all the holes for so long that you have forgotten that there are 10 other people waiting in the wings with fresh concrete, plaster, and paint.

It is no longer your job to be the flustered, emotional, and stressed business owner that does EVERYTHING for their brand. Delegation will set you free to become the calm, assertive, and inspiring leader that your employees have always wanted and needed.

Being the Big Picture Thinker

All successful business owners are big picture thinkers. The trick is that they do not only imagine these big pictures but they fill in the gaps and create implementable plans to get the business to that end goal point.

Most entrepreneurs dare to dream that one day their companies will earn millions and will have a staff of 500 people with 10 branches all over the country. Everyone has their own version of this dream. To bosses that use system thinking, these dreams are not dreams at all; they are attainable goals.

If you are not dreaming big for your company, who is? Who is actively planning and taking steps towards the growth and success of your business? No one, that is who! It is also the reason why you must implement x-treme distancing into your business culture.

Big picture thinkers drive businesses forward:

- Learn to identify patterns that emerge in business that cause consistent problems.
- Become an idea machine and a testing fanatic.
- Big thinkers do not engage in small, meaningless tasks.
- You are great at outlining a strategy, then slowly filling in the details.
- Be aware of your market, market trends, and fluctuations.
- Have one eye on your competition at all times.
- You develop an instinct for people you like to work with.

You are the only big thinker that your business will ever have, which is why it is up to you to assume this crucial role and expand your mind into new leadership areas. If you are not growing as a big picture thinker, then your business is not growing either.

As a boss, it is part of your job to develop your leadership abilities, business acumen, and skills as they pertain to the management and direction that your company needs. When you work IN your company, you do not give a second thought to developing your business skills. In fact, you barely even manage your staff.

How can you? You are too busy getting the work done. It can be pandemonium for the business owner that has trapped themselves inside their own business. This is your chance to free yourself and become the leader you were always meant to be.

Blueprint 3: The System Distancing Cycle

How exactly do you go about ensuring that you are remaining mechanically distant from your own company? By instituting a set of checks and balances and holding yourself accountable by involving your next-in-command.

- Systematically plan to hand over responsibility and authority for the tasks you do to other people in your business.

- If you need to, hire and train the best people for the job. They will not always fit into a position immediately, but with mentoring or adequate training, they may grow into their new roles and become assets to your company.

- Limit the time you spend at work. Arrive at 8 and get home by 5, or whatever your equivalent of a normal day may be. No more late hours, no more overworked you—it is that simple. Dial back your work hours.

- Create systems that teach your employees exactly how you like or prefer something to be done. Check that these systems are being followed instead of sitting there and doing them yourself, which is a big waste of your precious time.

- Start learning about leadership and business, and develop your skills as an ambitious leader—not as a business employee.

Changing Things up in Your Company

It may come as a surprise to your employees that you are handing over the bulk of the work to them. Explain that it is an emotional time for you and that you need their help to make the transition. Be friendly and engaging, and reinforce the fact that this change is for business growth, not business abandonment.

Your system distancing cycle needs to involve your new "persona" as the boss. That means being emotionally distant from your employees, respected, and obeyed. It means holding each and every employee accountable for the work they put out under your brand name.

Sit down right now and create your transition strategy. Moving from inside to outside your business is not easy, so document your progress. Reflect on the changes that you make—on what does and does not work. Find that balance, and start to be the leader that can grow your company far beyond anything you have previously imagined.

- Brainstorm, create, and implement a transition strategy. You are moving from working IN your business to working ON your business.
- Address the employees and get them on your side for these major changes. Explain and enforce the transition as a big thinking boss.

OPERATIONS MANAGEMENT

"In the end, all business operations can be reduced to three words: people, product, and profits."

LEE IACOCCA

How your business operates as an entrepreneur is often a secondary concern to things like income, expenses, and finding customers. When I did some investigations into small business operations, what I discovered was shocking.

A very big part of distancing yourself from your business physically and emotionally is linked to your ability to become a better operations manager. When you are in the thick of things, you simply cannot see where your core problems are.

The Business Operations Manual

Have you ever heard of a business operations manual? It is a way for bosses, business owners, and entrepreneurs to keep tabs on HOW their business is running—without having to live through any of the hard work.

There are three main goals that you need to achieve consistently if you are to become a better business operations manager. They are:

- To figure out how business operations can generate more income for you.

- To improve the asset value of your business.
- To secure and cement the income and therefore the value of your company.

Your job as a business leader is to become directly involved in the creation of your company's very own business operations manual. This will consolidate all of those areas that need work and outline the activities, procedures, processes, and rules that you put in place that govern how each part of your business is run.

A business plan is a great first step for an entrepreneur, but an operations manual is the collection of actionable routes to take to achieve the lofty goals laid out in your business plan. A wise entrepreneur constantly works on their operations manual, tweaking and adding to it as the months roll by.

- An operations manual will create a set of rules, standards, and practices for your company. It acts as your voice when you are not around.
- It results in better employees that are more productive. They know exactly what is expected of them, so they are able to make you happy all of the time.

Business operations manuals range from contact lists to checklists, policies, terms, processes, and guide inclusions. It all depends on how large and how detailed you want to go in deciding how systematized your business will become.

Business Culture, Business Law

Any business that is started shares the practices and values that you instill in the business culture. You and your employees believe that doing things a certain way makes for a better outcome, and these "things" need to be outlined in your operations manual.

As the newly distanced boss, your job is to create an attractive business culture that represents who you are and what you believe the right way to conduct business must be. This means detailing what you want your company to be like in an official document.

- Ask opinions from your employees.
- Foster new employee talent in your company.
- Share the responsibility and accountability with your managers.
- Always build on what the future could be like.
- Collect and review staff feedback.
- Inspire brand loyalty and employee happiness.
- Be innovative in everything that you do.
- Only hire people that fit in with your business culture.
- Team building and group consensus is important.
- Build on strengths and manage weaknesses; everyone has them.

Take some time to put together a list of things you want your business to exemplify. If I was a new employee in your company, how would I regard the way things look, feel, and are done in your business? This matters because you want to attract and retain good people.

Business culture can be shaped and developed over time, but you need to know all about business law right now. Having a legal advisor on the payroll is a good idea, even for small start-ups that only have less than 10 people in the company.

- You need to make sure everything and everyone is legal in your business. Legal fees, fines, and even jail time are a disaster and will affect your business culture.
- Knowing that your business is 100% legal and run properly will save you an enormous amount of time, money, and resources.

- Preparing for unexpected spot inspections, auditing, or investigations is an integral part of building a lasting, highly profitable company.

My advice would be to learn as much as you can about business law or to get a legal consultant for your business on retainer. These individuals will comb through your business and tell you if anything major is not in line with your legal system.

Business culture and business law are entwined because they both affect how your business operates. This is why both should be included in your business operations manual.

Promoting Talent in Operations

In any successful business model, the boss needs to make provision for talented individuals that choose to come and work for your company. During your many operational processes, you will see who is capable and worth nurturing for management positions or positions of leadership.

It is the worst mistake in the world to believe that your employees will be happy working for you forever with a set salary and no room for growth. People want the chance to be better, to be trained, and to be promoted—so you need a system for putting that in place.

Promotion talent based on an outline that you add to your operations manual is key to this link in the business success chain. Sustainability and opportunity really matter to employees, who have to incur the cost of living year after year.

- You do not want to spend time and money training employees so that they can leave and use their new skills somewhere else.
- You need to make the possibility for promotion very possible if certain criteria are met. Everyone in every position should understand how they could advance.

- Include sections on team dynamics, quality of work, innovation, leadership ability, creativity—and allow your team members to grow in the directions that they choose to grow in. When you try and limit staff members, they leave.

The Bureau of Labor Statistics recently reported that the average American worker stays in their job for a maximum of 4.4 years, with younger workers only remaining at their jobs for 3 years and inspiring a culture of job hopping. Talented employees go where they are appreciated and where there is room for growth and higher income.

Employees will always need motivation, and the ability to work towards a better life is exactly what you—as the boss—need to provide for them. Doing this early will ensure that you retain the talent that you train.

- Create a clearly defined process for how you decide to promote your employees, and then share it with them.
- Some of the best businesses in the world reward their best employees with recognition, higher pay, bonuses, incentives, and great job titles.

Something as small as a great job title can even be an inspiring thing to work towards. Mentioning to key employees that they could be up for promotion will also inspire them to work harder and better and to contribute more actively to your business culture.

Hitting Targets On Time Every Time

A very large part of implementing these corrective business systems involves instituting a culture of achievement—for you and your employees. Being able to "hit targets" is a skill that you need to integrate into every aspect of your company.

The very basis of operations management stems back to converting inputs like resources, materials, labor, and information into outputs, like services, and products in the most efficient way possible. It is important that you have a rolling target for every process that you create.

Building constant improvement into your business culture is a clever way of guaranteeing that your employees are always working smart and towards a tangible goal. Without these tangible goals, an employee can be average and go completely unnoticed.

- Simplify your core business operations, and break them down into tangible targets that you can run along a moving timeline. If your sales target for June is to earn another $10,000, then your team should be working towards that. Based on the outcomes, you can then reset the target for July.

- Always place a system of performance measurement in place so that you can gain a better understanding of how your current processes are working.

- You already have a batch of benchmark systems to try out. As you complete these over time, take note of how you can change and improve them. Get advice from the employees who are using your operations processes.

- Designate a meeting time every month to discuss how successfully your employees managed to achieve each operational target. Chat about the challenges, and come up with solutions for next month.

- All targets need to follow the SMART system—they should be specific, measurable, achievable, realistic, and set along a timeline. Targets are just consistent goals that must be met. If they are not met, there needs to be a very good reason.

Nurturing a business culture of reward and accountability is the best way to ensure that your employees are taking note of your business operations targets and meeting them consistently. Always reward the people who help you grow your business, and have a zero tolerance policy for people that fail to achieve what you have laid out.

If after a few months a sales team member is simply not hitting the numbers, then you have to let them go. You are losing income, and they are not performing. This is your business, and it rests on the shoulders of capable people and foolproof business systems.

Tools Assessment and Rediscovery

Operations management can take a long time to get right and a lifetime to perfect. It takes constant measurement, reassessment, team organization, and commitment—and, of course, the ability for your employees to hit the targets that you set.

There are many, many divisions in operations management that are simply too time consuming to employ without the help of adequate software. As I have mentioned before, implementing the right software systems into your business streamlines it from the beginning and rapidly improves your chances of success.

- Project management tools. Despite your niche field, your team probably needs one or more project management tools to cut back on time, resources, and financial investment. Projects need to be managed by you when you are at the office or away. Mobile connectivity is always best to have with all of your employees.

- Product development schedules. If you are building or manufacturing your own products, then you need software that will help you manage the process. From concept to the moment it rolls out of your factory, it all needs to be monitored.

- Maintenance policies. How can you improve your businesses maintenance policies while keeping all of your equipment in working condition? By including it into your tools assessment process. Schedule time in every so often to keep things in good condition, or you might have a serious problem down the line.

- Quality control and inspection. If your business is service-based, you need to make sure that your employees are keeping up with your operations manual outlines. This means seeing that every single system is working like clockwork according to a schedule. Pop in at unexpected times to do these checks; they matter.

As the boss, it is your job to continually make sure that your business is using the most affordable and the best software for operations management that is available today. You can even invest in software that helps you automate the policy enforcement process.

Take some time to research which software packages or tools may be useful for your business to use. There are many options, and they are sometimes niche specific. Depending on what it is that you need, focus on solving the core competencies that will get your business over the initial "re-structured" process.

Blueprint 4: The Operations Management Cycle

The operations management cycle has just become one of the most important parts of doing your job. As a business owner entrepreneur, you will need to implement and enforce these new operational goals from day 1.

- Create a complete operations manual. Do not forget to include your existing employees in this process, as they will have to carry out these new procedures and may have some valuable input to offer you.
- Build a business culture that inspires and promotes growth in all areas—especially for your employees. People love to

know that if they work hard, in a year they will be promoted and rewarded for that hard work.

- Get well acquainted with business law, and hire a legal consultant to assist you with making sure that all practices in your company are 100% legal. This will prevent any incidents or confusion as you expand aggressively later on.

- Promote talent in your business by instituting nurturing mentor programs or making it clear how ambitious employees can advance based on their input in your company. Those that want to succeed will work for your success, and you will both win!

- Learn to measure each and every result, and hit those targets when you set them. Creating a culture of goal achievement and improvement is exactly how you go from a 10-person business to a 100-person business in a few short years.

Hunting for the Right Tools and Operators

As you have probably figured out by now, software is key to systematizing your company. Alongside the software, however, is the staff that you need to train to use it. Otherwise, it will just be you sitting behind a computer NOT running your business again.

Reports need to be compiled on a weekly basis so that you stay in touch with exactly how your business is performing and how each employee is contributing to this performance. Spend a good amount of time finding the right software provider, and teach your employee managers how to use it and compile reports.

Set a time for these reports to be on your desk every week, and review them for the meeting later that day. This is how you as a business owner will now operate. Using evidence-based management, you will lead your business directly to growth and success.

SYSTEMS
MONEY
CYCLES

UNDERSTANDING
PROFITABILITY

"Profit in business comes from repeat
customers, customers that boast about
your project or service, and that bring
friends with them."

W. EDWARDS DEMING

Money is the reason that people like you and I got into building businesses in the first place. A business exists to make money. It affects absolutely every decision that you are going to make for the benefit of your company.

It is surprising, then, that so few business owners, CEOs, and executives miss the point of "the bottom line." In this third section of the MAXOut business methodology, you are going to learn why your attitude and practices with money have been misappropriated.

The Role of Money in Your Business

Money matters—we can all agree on that. So let's also agree that if you do not have enough money to run your business—let alone expand it—something is not right. The average, fiercely ambitious business person these days is all about the money.

It is just a shame that 95% of these go-getters are trusting a lot of superficial circumstances to get them from month to month. You handle the money—or your accountant does—and that is where it ends. Systematizing your money is probably the best thing you will ever do for your company. It does something critical, something you already feel like you are doing.

It lets you know, as the owner or person responsible, exactly what is happening with your business finances on a daily basis. Not monthly, not every now and then. Daily. This is one of the more difficult systems to put into place.

Make no mistake; it must happen. Gone are the days of "guessing" your way to "decent" books, losing money along the way through cracks in your "personal" system, and altering prices because of need instead of behaving like a financial institution.

Working with money in your business makes your business a financial institution in many ways. Would a bank drop prices suddenly to make more sales? Would they alter prices based on who they are selling to? Would they allow the line to hover on red—moments away from bankruptcy? No!

The role of money in your business is multi-faceted. It needs to PROVIDE for your business so that you always have what you need in order to sell. It also needs to EXPAND your business so that growth continues and income increases. If your money is failing to do either of these things, then it is time to systematize your money!

When It Comes In, When It Goes Out

I am going to ask you a question now that may shock you. Let it sink in for a moment before realizing just how much work needs to be done. That question is—"Do you know right now how much money comes in and goes out and where it is appropriated and how?"

Think about it. If you, as the owner, do not even know exactly what your business money is doing—down to the last penny—there is too much room for human error there. For all you know, you could be losing thousands of dollars on something someone else believes that you need, when in reality, you do not need it at all.

It is time to take responsibility for the money in your business. Now that you understand your role as a leader, be clear on this too.

A leader without resources cannot implement new ideas into their business.

In other words, you could assume your role as the leader, come up with a myriad of incredible ideas, and not be able to implement even one of them because you do not have any capital, or money, to work with. Sound familiar?

I understand that money is not the most fun part of business. It can be a slog wading through the tiny details of a sale, organizing invoices, or keeping track of stock inventory. There is nothing fun about money.

It makes complete sense then to systematize and automate your monetary processes. Imagine never having to draw up an invoice again, or deal with missing stock, or be short on cash because the month's books do not balance.

Instead, you need to look at what can be done to systemize these processes. Where do you get your money? How? Where does it go? How much do you lose to fees, expenses, payments, and bills? How do you keep track of all that money?

- Step 1 is finding a money management program that will help you systematize and automate your incoming and outgoing payments.
- From there, you will know how much money you need to bring in every day in order to make your monthly growth goal.
- You will also know exactly where your money goes and how much is needed just to cover your expenses.

If you are reading this and thinking, "Obviously, I have a great system in place," then wonderful! But chances are that you do not know enough about your business finances, that your "system" is not automated, and that your processes are outdated.

The Golden Rule of Cash Flow

A system money cycle is really how you will come to terms with the finances in your business. I will go into more detail about this later, but for now, let's talk cash flow. There is one thing that separates successful companies from failing, or ailing, companies.

Cash flow management is not only essential to your business; it is the only thing keeping you from going under. I was once told a little equation that made a lot of sense at the time. That equation was—in business—that 1-1 NEVER equals 2.

The premise behind this equation is simple. If your business is struggling and you have no cash flow, owners try to cut back on things in order to improve business. A franchisee, for example, will buy cheaper meat and less stock, do less advertising, and fire a staff member.

They subtract again and again from their business in the hope that it will eventually equal something MORE. This almost never happens! When you remove things that make your business great, it becomes worse. You have to sort out your processes and ADD to your business if you want to turn it around.

Having cash flow will prevent this scenario from ever happening. Cash flows in and out of your business all the time. There needs to be "cash on hand" for your business whenever you—as the ideas leader—need it.

If you have done your research and discovered that adding in two extra tables for your lunch time boom is worth the investment, there needs to be cash floating around to do that. Your business cannot function as a cash strapped person does.

People that are cash strapped are terrible with money. If your business is terrible with money, there is no point in keeping it open. This section is supposed to nail this down for you so that you really understand that businesses exist to make you money!

So what exactly is the golden rule of cash flow? It is simple—

there always needs to be a good, solid cash buffer between your business and its creditors. You should be able to stop running for a few months and still be in the green. A year is the commonly accepted time.

Every month your cash flow needs to increase or compound. You should be able to purchase things that you need for new ideas, investments, or growth opportunities. Makes sense, right? Too often I consult for a business that can barely afford to stay open at all; their debts are astronomical, and they have zero cash flow.

The Scale Trap: How to Grow

Money leads to growth. As I was explaining in the cash flow section, there will be times when you want to expand your business in new directions or try new revenue streams. These can be risky, and they may succeed or fail right away. Testing is the only way to find out.

All great business owners or CEOs take these risks based on both growth potential and cash investment. These will impact the business over time depending on how you choose to manage your money.

A business with a systematized and automated money management system will know exactly how much cash to spend on a new venture according to legitimate figures from past earnings. Essentially, you should be able to implement these new growth opportunities, fail miserably, and not take any financial backlash from it.

Business owners that sell the most test the most. Everyone's industry is different, so when it comes to expansion, there is no black and white plan for you to implement. A lot of it will need to be learned based on risks that you take.

Business expansion is a trap for a lot of business owners. They spend all of their time building their business then running it—

that they forget that the goal is income and expansion. If your business is not growing, it is not moving forward. Only successful businesses grow. There is no such thing as a stagnant successful business.

Startup mode is over—your competition is already growing, expanding, and dipping their toes into new areas. If you are going to keep up, you have to be willing to incur the risk. Whether this means opening a second location, turning your business into a franchise, licensing your products, diversifying your sales portfolio, or targeting new markets, it must be done.

As you have just learned, however, growth is impossible without adequate money management, a consistent cash flow cycle, and—of course—a business leader with new ideas. And this is what most businesses sorely lack, which is why they fail to expand.

The good news is that with the Internet, anyone can afford to grow in new directions with minimal costs to begin with. Even the most cash-strapped, deep-in-debt company can sort out their finances to a point where in their immediate future, they can afford to invest in online marketing or sales. You must grow all the time—even if it is just a little bit each month.

The 80/20 Business Investment Process

What if I told you that your business is not your own private source of money? I once mentored a small business owner that sold food out of a food truck. She could not understand why she was not making any money when she had tried everything.

Immediately I assessed the problem—she was treating the truck business as her personal bank account instead of allowing her business to be an "individual" in its own right. Businesses need money too—to run, to grow, and to eventually succeed.

Even the smallest, struggling business can repair its finances if they begin to treat their businesses like "people" that deserve a salary. I asked her, "How much money do you pay your business to work for you?" She did not understand me at first.

I went on to explain that a business can only improve when it has its own money. Remember that cash flow, year-long stash I was talking about? This is how you start to build it! I used the 80/20 rule, but you can make it a variation of this rule according to what you can afford.

Basically, once the expenses are covered and the profit is calculated, you need to make one final payment to build the capital equity and worth of your business. For every 80% of that profit that is used for repairs, maintenance ideas, and other stuff, 20% should be placed into a fixed account.

The more money you can "stash" into that account, the safer your business will be. Learning how to invest in the growth of your own business is as simple as putting 20% of your net profit away each month. That money belongs to your business. It will keep it alive, and it will get it through any hard times that may throw a pebble in the works in the future.

It is not only about generating more cash flow and experimenting more with innovative ideas—it is also about dividing your profit and re-investing it in the entity that is your business. By the end of the first year of doing this, you may have enough to comfortably hire another person or even a team of people depending on your profit. Now that is growth!

Blueprint 5: The Profitability Cycle

Profit, like marketing, does not just happen. There is far too much choice in this world of ours. There are dozens of ways that profit can become derailed if you let it.

That is why you have to find the right information, make the right decisions, establish the best processes, and decide on the right compensation plan. This all begins with systematizing your money.

- Source a great financial management software package, and make a plan to invest in it as soon as you can.

- Take a look at running a personal finance package alongside your business finance software so that you can keep tabs on both. Often business owners' personal money mingles too much with their business finances.

- Find a couple of apps that you can use on your smartphone to help you effectively manage things like stock control and invoicing, and set up a feedback and notification system that sends you reports daily, updating you on your financial situation.

- These reports can contain automated goals that you have pre-set and that will give you a daily or weekly target to work towards. All income needs to be centered on plans for future growth and ideas testing.

I will go into much more detail about putting together your profit cycle strategies later on in the book. For now, start thinking about these important questions:

- Do you know what comes in daily, weekly, and monthly?

- Do you know what goes out daily, weekly, and monthly?

- Can you account for every penny that flows through your business?

- How much can you afford to put into a fixed business bank account (the 20%)?

- Do you stop managing your money once it has become profit?

- Do you know where your profit goes?

- What systems could you put in place for streamlining the incoming/outgoing cash system in your business?

- How can you make this system safer, faster, leak-proof, and an instrumental tool for your overall monthly success?

- Do you have ideas for business growth that you would like to implement?
- How can you create the cash flow to get yourself to that point?
- Are you afraid to take risks in business because if you fail you will hurt your company?
- How could you brainstorm a way to minimize risk, increase cash flow, and adequately divide your profit into appropriate areas?

THINKING
AHEAD

"What lies behind us and what lies
ahead of us are tiny matters compared
to what lives within us."

HENRY DAVID THOREAU

The second part of working with money in your business is about thinking ahead. Money can drag the average business owner back into the past because of unpaid debt. It also has the ability to make you very fearful about moving forward.

This actually prevents you from thinking ahead and hoping and planning your way out of a bad financial situation. It all begins with a different mindset—you control money; it does not control you. Let's see how you can better get a grip on this concept.

Tapping the Global Online Market

What is in the cards for your business in the next year? Do you have growth plans, or are you living from month to month? It is sad that so many businesses fail to see that money (or lack of money) is holding them prisoner.

This line of thought may have been applicable ten years ago, but today it is only an excuse. With the World Wide Web transforming small businesses into global empires faster than anything we have seen in human history, the onus is on you to take advantage of this resource.

It simply does NOT matter what niche you are in or what kind of business you run. You have your local customers, and you have millions more online. I have watched hundreds of businesses successfully expand into the online space.

Financially, the overheads are minimal, and with enough time and effort, you can learn to leverage the Internet, social media, and content marketing for the benefit of your business. Couple this with a sound financial plan, and nothing will hold you back.

- If you own a service business, you will be booked 24/7.
- If you own a product-based business, you will sell more than ever before.

Technology is nothing to be feared; it should be embraced and seen for what it is—a chance for you to quickly expand your business without having to incur the costs of new premises, staff, or overheads. Done correctly, it could more than quadruple your income in one year.

You need to tap into the global online market so that you can access a readily available source of income for your business that is lying in wait for your online presence. If you do not have a website, blog, or social media or content marketing strategy just yet, look into it.

The Flexibility Mindset

Many business executives or owners are stuck in a perpetual mental rut. The struggle of working hard constantly and keeping things going is incredibly draining. It is only a matter of time before your own business is one of the most stressful things in your life.

When stress, lack of money, and constant work creep up on you, your mindset suffers. You become naturally inflexible because every part of your brain is already firing on all cylinders. There is simply no brain power left to dedicate to any kind of outside, foreign, or "new" way of thinking. The person at the center of a maze has no idea what the maze looks like. They can only pace back and forth, desperately trying to find their way out!

Instead, I encourage all of my clients to adopt the flexibility mindset. A business owner that has systematized their money and distanced themselves from their company is perfectly poised to invest in exciting new ways of thinking.

The ability to shift your thoughts, see things from new perspectives, and be able to identify new opportunities or ideas because of it is what you want to achieve. Flexible thinking uses your emotions, actions, and motivations for the benefit of your business.

For example, if the sale of cupcakes has not been working out, you may want to try a few different methods before scrapping the idea. The process may involve asking customers to try samples and getting feedback then integrating this feedback into the cupcake recipe.

Be flexible enough with your thinking; everything from placement, price, decoration, theme, size, packaging, and design can affect the sale. With flexible thinking, any poorly selling product or service can be turned around. I really believe that. It is just a matter of reframing and repurposing the process.

- To develop a more agile mind, focus on changing the context of your line of thought. Try new things, question your motives, be spontaneous, and—of course—always get the opinion of others. More on crowdsourcing success later in the chapter!

A flexible mindset does not see money as something that imprisons but rather something that will set you free. If you cannot find the solution, it does not mean that it does not exist—it just means that you need help, or a different mindset, to find it. When it comes to money, this can be an indispensable trait to nurture.

"New" Is Always on the Go

There are a lot of business lessons that I have learned from the online space. For example, brands tend to redesign their logos and update their websites a LOT. I would say at least once a year, maximum once every two years. Why is that?

The Internet is a massive global feedback system that has been proven. People, as it turns out, like "new." Products that contain the word "new" on it sell more than products that do not. A freshly opened store does better in the first few months because it is new.

It seems as though the world just loves relevant, up to date, cutting edge, forward thinking companies. And that is why you need to be one. I am not talking about revamping your look or spending thousands on your "image"—though you should consider it down the line.

What I am talking about is much more valuable. Have you noticed how business today is incredibly different from business 20 to 30 years ago? There is a good reason for that! The business market is different. People are different. Our circumstances have changed.

Your financial situation has the best chance of improving right away if you understand that there will always be an element of "new" that you have to pursue in business: new ways of systematizing things, new software programs, and new online platforms to learn about.

You cannot expect to take a business model from 30 years ago that completely discounts technology and expect to stay ahead in your industry. It is not going to happen. We live in a highly dynamic, changing world these days.

More books and information are being published than ever before. Better yet—your customers are actually reading all of this information and evolving. They want different things and are no longer the passive, geographically challenged individuals they once were.

So lose the idea that business can only happen in one particular way. This is wrong, and it will cripple you over time. Business can be done in a number of different ways. Your job is to stay abreast of what is happening in your field and be the better version of what people want in order to inspire more business revenue.

New does not mean old and stagnant. New is always on the move. New looks for ways to keep improving, changing, and adapting. This kind of culture in your business will inflate your profit to heights you never believed possible in your niche.

Crowdsourcing Business Success

In the online and offline space, you are at the mercy of a buying public that is exposed to thousands of advertising messages every month. They have the power and the ability to buy from anyone at any time.

Why would they buy from you? What makes your business different? These are the eternal questions that evolve along with your business and the income that it is able to make. Low income means that people are choosing NOT to buy from you.

The good news is that a wise business owner will invest in business success by FINDING out what their customers want. Everything from products, services, and experiences can be sourced from your very own community or buying public.

I once had to bring a barber shop owner back to the real world by going out into the street and collecting opinions from random "passersby" on what his shop was like. They were not good, and the owner was completely surprised to hear them! We can often be blinded to the truth, which is why getting your customer opinions is so crucial to your profit cycle.

- Implement systems that collect feedback from customers in real-time, using apps or simple survey machines or forms.

- Build a community on the Internet, and then crowdsource feedback from this community to find out what they think about each and every experience that they have inside your business or with your business.

The only way you will ever know how your business is perceived is to actively collect the data, analyze it, and create a set of insights that can be used to spur positive action. The "crowd" has just become your greatest financial asset.

Imagine if you could give every customer that you dealt with the ideal experience working with your business or purchasing your products. I bet that your business would take off simply by word of mouth. That is what you want for your company.

The only way to quickly and effectively ramp up your sales is to formulate a set of crowdsourcing business success systems. You need to grab the data and use it to streamline what you offer to your customers.

Improving Systems Management

Once all of your systems have been put into place, you will need a way to manage them that ensures they never break down. Remember that these systems make it easy for any employee to work for your business in exactly the right way.

The success lies in the system, not in the employee. It makes sense then that systems management should be a key role in your business. Someone has to make sure that all of your carefully planned and implemented systems run like clockwork.

This can fall to the manager to do, but you should also take an active role in it. After all, you are the boss, and you decide how things are run. Your systems guarantee success, but you need to empower the people that you hire in order to keep these systems running.

- Create a benchmark system so that you know where to begin.

- Implement a feedback system so that you are aware of the areas that need improvement.
- Run system tests to see which versions work best.
- Collect customer, employee, and leadership feedback, and take it all into account when analyzing your data.
- Make decisions about adjusting your systems once you have drawn insights from the data, feedback, and tests.
- Output the new system, and test every three to six months.

A simple process like this will ensure that you constantly improve your systems at every level. From hiring a new employee, to generating invoices, to making a specific product sale, to executing a certain service—there should be a system in place for everything.

Systems thinking is how you consistently improve your existing systems once they have been implemented and are working for the success of your business. To improve systems management in your company, you have to make someone accountable for it.

I suggest all levels of management be accountable, and then ultimately you should have the final say or sign-off. This will also leave you room to nurture leaders inside your business who will happily work for your success if they are properly motivated financially. A whole world will open up to you when you sort out your money systems!

Blueprint 6: The Systems Progress Cycle

Money is supposed to grow so that your business can expand. The only way to guarantee that this happens is by sorting out the issues I have spoken about in this chapter. For this money blueprint, you need to focus on progress.

A systems progress cycle is supposed to ensure that your systems never go out of date so that your business is able to continually serve your customers in the best way possible. Running like clockwork is time sensitive. There will always be better practices and processes that can significantly improve your revenue if you let them.

To begin the blueprint process, ask yourself these questions:

- How can you make innovation a big part of your business systems?
- Which areas do you predict will require revamping more often than others?
- How much research do you do for every customer experience?
- How much time do you invest in developing new ideas?
- Think about a process that you can track, develop, and improve revenue on.
- Ask friends, employees, family, and customers for feedback.
- Do you really know what people think of your business?
- How much strategic planning have you done for your business systems to date?
- Do you get weekly reports that update you on various sectors in your business?

In order for your business to move forward and progress, you must gain control of your financial situation via competent money system cycles. Only when you establish these measureable systems will you know where and how you can improve your revenue streams.

It all starts with you, your systems, and how you plan on continually developing them until you reach that point where your business is successful enough to sell (for retirement) or automated enough to continue earning great money for you with little personal investment.

- How can you improve your income?
- Where can you improve your income?
- How often will you tweak your established systems?

Your job is now this—to manage the systems and the people that run your systems. You need to see your business from a bird's eye view in order to expand it successfully. With a focus on the customer, on profit, and on expansion, you will excel.

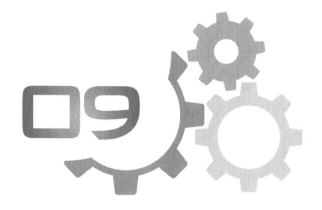

BLUEPRINT 1: THE SYSTEM MEASUREMENT CYCLE

"A point of view can be a dangerous luxury when substituted for insight and understanding."

MARSHALL MCLUHAN

How do you go about establishing systems that can be measured consistently? The answer to that question depends on your niche, your role, and the amount of time you are willing to dedicate to the success of each freshly implemented system.

A system measurement cycle is a way to consistently develop, grow, and maintain how you measure your business—and in which key areas you will find the most room for return. The goal here is to keep these five strategy areas updated at all times.

The FLIC Measurement Cycle

The FLIC measurement cycle is a process that I have created that will help you measure the areas that matter most to your bottom line on a regular, systemized basis.

FLIC literally stands for:

- Financial Measurement
- Learning and Growth Strategy
- Internal Business Measurement
- Customer Measurement

These are the four core areas or KPIs (key performance indicators) that you will need to focus on in order to effectively maintain systems measurement in your company:

- *Financial Measurement Strategy:* The first step in the measurement cycle is to implement a system of financial measurement. You need to know what is coming in, what is going out, and how to appropriately portion money to the right areas.

- *The Learning and Growth Strategy:* The second step in the measurement cycle is to focus on implementing personal systems of measurement. How are you improving and evolving as a business leader? How can your actions be measured?

- *The Internal Business Measurement Strategy:* The third step in the measurement cycle is to measure the internal results that your business produces. What is the data saying? Which systems produce certain results?

- *The Customer Measurement Strategy:* The fourth step in the measurement cycle focuses on your customers. How do you measure their interactions with your company? How can you collect data on the ways your customers feel?

- *Reporting and Decision Making:* Once all of the data has been sorted into various analytics programs for analysis and insight generation, you will need to compile reports for review. These will help you make actionable decisions that will affect positive change in your company.

The System Measurement Cycle hones in on the four core areas that make it possible to run a business successfully—money, leadership, operations, and customer service—and it devises a way for you to consistently measure them for improvement.

The Financial Measurement Strategy

In order to implement a measurement strategy in your business, you will need to identify the right tools and then assign the maintenance of these tools to a particular person.

1. Find the right financial software package. Conduct research on NetSuite or Quicken to systematize and automate your daily finances.
2. Identify the correct person to work with this program. Your in-house accountant, secretary, or business manager are options.

Once you have done this, you will need to go through a period of training (yourself and the individual that will be working with the software). During this process, you will establish which key components you want inserted into your weekly (then monthly) reports.

- Keep in mind if you already have software, you are looking to upgrade. Measurement is about finding the best offering out there to simplify your business finances.

From here, you will need to establish benchmarks. That means finding out how your business has been doing financially until now. If it has been open for six months or five years, you are about to see how well you have been managing the money side of your company.

Find the answers to each of these strategic KPIs:

- What are your weekly expenses?
- What is your weekly income?
- Your net profit—what are you left with after all expenses and costs are closed?

- Your net profit margin—how does your profit compare to other companies like yours?
- Operating profit margin—what is the operating income vs. operating costs of your business?
- Revenue growth rate—start tracking how much your income grows each month.
- Cash conversion cycle—what is the time it takes to turn resources into cash flow?
- Your break-even point—find out what it is and when it is every month.
- Net cash flow—subtract cash inflows and outflows.

These can be expanded upon in significant detail until you are producing quarterly reports that chart your measurement progress. This is about capturing the data in ways that are practical and usable for your business.

Once you have established your benchmark data based on your present and past history, it is important to create a REALISTIC projection of what your finances may look like in the coming year, if you plan on growing them.

- Identify key milestones from your financial data.
- Develop a list of potential tasks that need funding for revenue growth.
- Establish your investment plan—how much money will you give to your business so that it can grow in equity value and worth?
- Create a policy for financial measurement that will govern your processes for producing these numbers every day, week, and month.

The Learning and Growth Strategy

The second step of the FLIC measurement cycle involves your own personal learning and growth as a business owner. As you have discovered in this book, the only way to keep a business moving forward and gaining in success is to be a good leader.

This is why it is important to continue your own growth experiences by focusing on areas where you may need help. Any number of these could improve your business.

- Additional education in a specific field: finance, business management, marketing
- Foundation knowledge and understanding of technology and the digital marketplace
- Gaining additional insight by formulating a list of business books and then reading them
- Networking with other people facing the same challenges in your niche
- Involving your business in the local community

There are some excellent ways to motivate yourself to become a better, stronger, more powerful business leader. Take a look at your current salary. If you want a much larger one, then work with your finances and set goals. If you can reach X, then you can give yourself an increase. Constantly relate your personal growth with your business's financial growth.

- Take classes in personal development as a business leader.
- Learn to speak in front of people, and become a respected member of society.
- Develop your ability to think critically and creatively.
- Learn about better decision making and what it means for you.

To execute this, there will be four areas that you need to focus on constantly. They are leadership growth, educational expansion, reputation, and societal impact.

- *Leadership growth:* In your own personal capacity, you will need to read as many business books as you can. Learn practical lessons as well while working on growing who you are as a business leader.

- *Educational expansion:* Learn more! Take courses, study new subjects, or finally do that six-week introduction to online marketing. Always grow in what you are able to learn.

- *Reputation:* How do your customers and employees perceive you? Actively work on expanding a reputation in your business with your competitors, community, and providers. People need to know you are fair, competent, and someone to be respected.

- *Societal impact:* Giving back to your community is a key part of business growth. If you are not engaging with the community, they will forget about you. Always find ways to give back and to grow along with the people that support your business goals.

Establish your own personal priorities for learning and growth!

The Internal Business Measurement Strategy

Your third step is to implement an internal business measurement strategy that will help you determine how efficiently your business runs. Operations are at the heart of any business, and you will be surprised to know just how much time, effort, and vision is wasted on the wrong areas. This section is about formulating a strategy that will keep you on track.

- *Review all of your practical processes.* Review, modify, and deploy benchmark operational measures.

- *Review people.* Set benchmarks for employee performance, and devise a way to improve these performance measures each month.

- *Review systems.* Operations all depend on the systems that you have implemented. It is your job to review existing systems and to improve them consistently—even if it takes a period of a few months.

- *Review the business culture.* In operations, what your business stands for is paramount. Establish a systems management culture in your business to make sure that operations never stagnate or stop improving.

You will want to focus on performance, time management, revenue, and efficiency in this section. All of these will help you improve operations in your business. Learn to look at your business from an internal perspective to set strategic priorities.

- View your business from the outside—like a customer or shareholder might. Where do you see opportunities for improvement? Document these, and formulate a strategy for testing and implementing new systems based on an operational perspective.

- From strategic goals, improvement objectives, action plans, and performance measures, you should be able to gain a greater understanding of your company.

All of these should be developed by asking where you want to go and where you need to go along with how you are going to get there. Tactical plans can then be established that will result in these measureable actions.

- To establish measurable systems in operations, you will combine data collected from your business processes, people, systems, and culture. From there, you will identify opportunities, establish growth points, and make positive changes.

- To move from what you have now to what you want, you will need to take a strategy like this and apply it to your business, breaking it down into smaller tactics that become your own scalable and measurable action plans.

- These actions plans must be specific, measurable, date-specific, assigned, linked, feasible, and monitored by a senior staff member. Problem solving is your new mantra, and getting from your sluggish systems to your newly established, fast-paced, highly efficient systems will require everyone's involvement.

The Customer Measurement Strategy

Customers may not always be right, but they are always supposed to be at the center of every business decision that you make. Measuring how satisfied your customers are with your business is very important in the growth and expansion of your company revenue.

That is why in this fourth section of the FLIC measurement cycle, you will need to establish a measurement strategy to keep tabs on your customer satisfaction.

- How can you improve customer retention?
- How can you attract more customers?
- How can you improve the customer experience in every way?

Here is how your company should measure customer satisfaction:

- Overall emotional satisfaction should be broken down into three contexts: overall quality, perceived reliability, and the extent of their needs fulfilled.
- Measure their loyalty in both affective and behavioral contexts. How satisfied are they with your brand? How likely are they to buy again? Would they recommend your brand to people they know and love?

- Measure more specific satisfaction goals according to the thing you are asking them about. For example, a product might invite feedback on taste, presentation, packaging, and price.

- Measure their intent to return and purchase again from you. This can be done in a variety of ways, but the key here is to bring people back—any way that you can.

There are many ways to gain data from customers—using online marketing, in-store feedback systems (like machines), apps, or surveys. By far the most efficient way is to have an app created for your brand.

In-store and online users could then use this app to provide real-time feedback for your brand. Build it into a rewards system to improve their loyalty, and people will gladly help you build the best customer service business you can imagine.

If you work in an office environment, you can also use social media to collect and analyze customer complaints and feedback, though this should be kept to a minimum. In fact, evidence suggests that having an app where people can complain keeps your social media properties free of harsh complaints unless they are really serious.

I would also consider working a monitoring strategy into this area so that you can keep your ear to the ground on sites like Yelp, where open, public criticism and reporting can lose you a lot of business.

Reporting and Decision Making

Now that you have a basic plan for each of your four measurement strategies, you should also know that these are the areas where you will be receiving weekly reports. As the boss or business owner, it is not up to you to keep the measurement system going.

It is your job, however, to read the reports and hold your employees accountable when the numbers, surveys, or new systems to not produce results. It should all be there for you to see each and every week. At the end of the month, you should receive an overall report that includes the trends and results from the previous six months to a year on it.

- Weekly finance measurement reports will help you see which days need work.
- Monthly finance measurement reports help you contextually improve your revenue.
- Weekly learning and growth reports keep you on track as a business owner.
- Monthly learning and growth reports show you how much progress you are making.
- Weekly internal business reports are used to see how operations are performing daily.
- Monthly internal business reports will show you the month in context.
- Weekly customer reports keep you aware of service and experience concerns.
- Monthly customers reports help you monitor service quality in context.

As you can see here, reporting really helps your business in two specific ways:

- The first is that by receiving weekly reports, you can fully understand problems and concerns as they arise and adjust them to prevent future problems.
- The second is that by receiving monthly reports, you can compare them to previous months in context to get a better view of the overall picture.

As a competent business owner, these measurement reports will help you keep a closer eye on the micro-details of your business and on the macro-details that drive revenue. Instituting a new measurement-based reporting system can be a challenge, but it is very worth it.

- Reports do not have to be long. They only have to contain the various KPIs that you have established, along with a small paragraph or two write-up of any incidents or issues that occurred that week.

- These reports will be used in the monthly meeting, where everyone is held accountable for the numbers and progress of the business. With hard data and a way to improve the measurement of systems in your company, you can work with your team to develop clear solutions for the following month.

BLUEPRINT 2: THE SYSTEM AUTOMATION CYCLE

"As technology advances, it reverses the characteristics of every situation again and again. The age of automation is going to be the age of 'do it yourself.'"

MARSHALL MCLUHAN

One of the most important keys to any successful business these days is automation—whether you are doing it online or in the real world. With the MAXOut System Methodology, you will be required to implement automation strategies for continued success.

This means that you will create a process cycle made up of various automation strategies that you maintain consistently in a long-term capacity.

BOBS Automation Cycle

The BOBS automation cycle is created from a set of strategies that will help you establish and build automated processes and systems into your current business. These strategies will ensure that your company stays on track despite environmental changes.

BOBS stands for:

- **B**usiness Rules Automation Strategy
- **O**nline Reputation Strategy
- **B**usiness Process Automation Strategy
- **S**ilo Re-Engagement Strategy

These four core areas will act as key performance indicators as you implement, adjust, and improve your various business systems.

- *The Business Rules Automation Strategy:* When you know the rules of your own business, it makes decision making easy. Processes are managed better when there are clear automated rules governing various parts of your business.
- *The Online Reputation Strategy:* What people think of your brand or business online matters, which is why you need a method of automating your marketing efforts. When you can automate and control your marketing, you can control how people perceive you on the Internet.
- *The Business Process Automation Strategy:* This is a strategy that your business will use to automate processes in order to keep costs down. It involves using technology, repositioning your staff, and integrating new methods of application.
- *The Silo Re-Engagement Strategy:* This is a method of automation that involves working with the employees of your company in order to make everyone equally responsible for various processes and outcomes in your business. No more silos!
- *Reporting and Decision Making:* The final step will be to put together reports that you can review on the state of your automation systems. These will help you plan for the new month, correct what has been going wrong, and engage in automation opportunities when they arise.

Your BOBS system automation cycle will work to keep your rules, reputation, processes, and employees moving in the right direction—so that your business can excel.

The Business Rules Automation Strategy

Your new business rules automation strategy consists of two main components. These will help you govern the operational efficiency of systems that do not have to be constantly watched by employees but do have to be carefully monitored by them.

- The first component is finding software that will help you with decision automation based on the rules that you have created for your business.
- The second is to recruit someone within your company to work with this system and keep it up to date.

Automating your business rules leads to the ability to partially automate your decisions—which has far reaching positive consequences for your business. You will be able to manage complexity, ambiguity, compliance, and agility—all while making faster, safer decisions.

As part of business process management, you can see how knowing exactly how to run your business would be beneficial. It gives you the room to communicate these rules to a software program that will then assist you in enforcing and recovering data based on these decisions. The result is cost efficiency and less time spent on decision making.

- Remember that the business rules that you create will become an asset for your company and will include how you operate, do business, make decisions, and perform many other vital functions.

Why Bother Automating Business Rules?

Your business already operates based on a set of rules you implemented some time ago. When you do not have an automated system that captures how rules are treated, implemented, and changed in your company, you will not improve.

It is the very over-arching principle of running a successful company that the rules be flexible and easy to roll out accurately, consistently, and widely to all areas of your company. This makes sure that varied expertise is applied in the right areas, even when you are not around. The software that you use will give you great insight into how you really do business.

Find an automated business rules software package. Work with your team to input your solid business rules, and make sure everyone has access to them.

Appoint an individual, specifically a senior manager, to take care of business rules automation. You will need a monthly report on how effectively people in your business are using these rules and making decisions based on them.

The Online Reputation Strategy

What people say about your brand online matters. But let's be honest; no one has time to sit and work on your online brand identity for hours and hours every day. So to solve the disconnect between potential customer perspective and who you are, employing a marketing automation system is required.

- Your marketing automation system will find you new customers and help you retain and nurture your existing customers for greater profit.

Marketing automation allows you to work smarter—focusing more on how your business runs and engages with your customers in the real world instead of having to dedicate large amounts of time to online marketing (and not very good online marketing!).

- Find the best possible marketing automation software, and work on integrating it into your business. Setup can take time, but once it is done, you will only need to dedicate a few hours every month to your marketing automation practice.
- Sit down with a qualified marketing professional that works

for you, and discuss goal setting. Decide on the goals that you want to set for your marketing automation based on the first month and then every three months after that.

- The individual that you choose to run your marketing software must be able to create a checklist for you so that you can see what they are doing with your marketing automation software on a weekly basis.

Initially, you can begin with a basic email marketing campaign, newsletters, and perhaps some SMS marketing. Only use marketing automation software that deploys and tracks your campaign progress. It is pointless if you are not going to be able to collect and analyze data.

If you can find a software program that integrates with social media, that is even better. Content marketing and social media will eventually become key areas that you will need to address in order to stay competitive in your niche. For now, a basic social campaign is a good start. You should also look into creating a blog and using it as your content springboard.

- Software should be able to deploy to a multitude of touch points : desktop, email, mobile phones, tablets, iPods, and other devices.
- Marketo, Eloqua, Hubspot, SimplyCast, Pardot, Genius, and InfusionSoft are all viable marketing automation systems.

At the end of every week your marketing automation manager should be able to automatically create reports that will compile your stats and data for some light weekend reading. This will help you stay afloat in terms of getting the word out about your brand.

The Business Process Automation Strategy

Business process automation is all about finding out what parts of your business can be automated and how. It is key to properly systematizing your business by first stripping away the parts that you do not have to handle yourself and then focusing on what must be managed, streamlined, reworked, and elaborated upon.

Many business processes can be automated, and it will save you time, money, and resources in the long run. Administration, for example, is a time consuming task; it is far better to simply automate the process. Anything done on paper can be automated. It will change the way you do business forever; plus, machines rarely make errors!

- Source a good quality business process automation software package. Often business rules software may be integrated with a BPM package.

- Business process management is basically software data collaborating with expertise from people within your company to control all core business processes. You must find a manager that is willing to take on this responsibility.

- Once you have found your manager and software, it will be a testing process. Within this context, you can streamline business processes, assign tasks to people, regulate compliance with business rules, choreograph systems, and integrate internal practices with external marketing goals.

Once you have settled on your IT infrastructure, the process is relatively straightforward. As usual, you will need to set goals so that you know how you are going to go about establishing these systematized processes.

All business processes can become strategic assets if you work on them for long enough. Management and processing of information is your job as the boss, the CEO, or the owner. This information needs to be governed and managed by your managers and teams before they can supply you with this detailed information every week and every month.

- Improve productivity using BPM systems
- Increase revenue using BPM systems
- Decrease costs using BPM systems
- Implement and streamline systems with BPM goals

Imagine if ordering stock was done automatically and that your finances were managed automatically so that the stock would always be paid for on time. The amount of money you would save on late payments alone is impressive, not to mention improved supplier relations, better customer service, and smooth business operations.

All BPM software needs to be customized to a certain extent. When you purchase that software, however, there will be support teams available to you. It is very common for software companies to assist in the initial setup of your software.

The Silo Re-Engagement Strategy

In a silo re-engagement strategy, you are working towards a holistic perspective of business instead of a narrow, siloed perspective that has led to so many problems in small- and medium-sized businesses. When everyone is accountable for the tasks they are assigned to, the business just runs better.

- Consider linking your employees to your main software systems. For example, a point of sale system these days allows waiters and waitresses to have their own touch screen mobile device that tracks their sales for the day.

How Do I Go About Implementing This Strategy?

Sit down with your employees and discuss how you can better communicate with each other in your business in order to advance the company from fresh perspectives. The senior manager should have a direct line to even the most insignificant dish washer.

This strategy treats your people as human assets and uses them as an innovative feedback method for the benefit of your business systems. Automating this process means making it part of your business culture to be innovative in any job you are in.

That means actively trying to come up with ways to make things faster, better, more efficient, less time consuming, and more engaging for the customer. If all of your employees are concerned, not just with their pay checks but with growing your business, you will succeed.

Gone are the days of siloed departments that do not talk to each other. Who knows how much better off your business would be if finance teams spoke to marketing divisions or creative teams spoke to business leadership. You need a multitude of perspectives in order to run a successful, modern company—and everyone needs to be accountable.

- Create a basic system of "encouragement" or "incentive" to get your employees to begin thinking of ways they can help the business. All suggestions are welcome, but only one every week (or month) will be chosen.

- Make time to get to know your employees. They are the people you are trusting with your financial future. You would be surprised how many owners do not even know who is working for them or why. Re-engage!

You can automate this process by setting business outings for you and your team at least once a month. Reward the individuals that actively show that they want to help your business become successful. Fire the individuals that only want to collect a paycheck. This is your life—if your business is failing, often it is because your people do not care!

Reporting and Decision Making

If you can manage to find the right software providers and recruit the right managers, then you should expect a report each week from each of these four core automated systems. Yes! I said all four—even your silo re-engagement strategy.

As the owner, these changes may come as a shock to your staff. Business automation, however, will make their jobs easier so they will be willing to help. Collecting these reports is essential to the success of your business.

- Weekly business rules automation reports will show you how your rules affect your average day.
- Monthly business rules automation reports help you see where you can improve.
- Weekly online reputation reports keep your online marketing earning for you.
- Monthly online reputation reports: Shows you where you need to invest online
- Weekly business process automation reports monitor system performance.
- Monthly business process automation reports refine successful systems.
- Weekly re-engagement reports inspire your employees to innovate.
- Monthly re-engagement reports show you where your employee issues are.

Just by glancing at the brief reasons to keep these reports coming in, you can see what a huge impact these automated system reports will have on your decisions.

Not only will you understand how your business operates and why but you will also communicate this to the World Wide Web, implement and improve quality systems, and improve on your human asset potential.

More specifically, these reports will:

- Help you streamline the way your business is run.
- Help you discover and retain new customers and sources of revenue.
- Assist you in creating, implementing, improving, or removing systems.
- Show you how to nurture people as part of your company.

Automation was designed to help business owners concentrate on the more important areas of their business. Once technology has taken over, it leaves your employees wide open. From there, you will be able to see who deserves rewards and who does not.

When people cannot hide behind faulty systems and poor decision management, it makes for a very honest presentation of how they are affecting your company. Not only will systems automation cycles like this keep you gaining in revenue and success but they will help you avoid individuals that actively pull your company into the mud. No one needs that!

BLUEPRINT 3: THE SYSTEM DISTANCING CYCLE

"Our main business is not to see what lies dimly at a distance, but to do what lies clearly at hand."

THOMAS CARLYLE

Your third blueprint connects with your own involvement in your business. As the owner or boss, you need to redefine your role so that it is abundantly clear, not only to you but to everyone that works for you.

A system distancing cycle will help you systematize how you respond to your business and how your employees respond to you. This may be one of the most important cycles in the MAXOut System Methodology, so do not ignore it!

The PICE Distancing Cycle

I call this the PICE Distancing Cycle, and I created it to help you reprioritize the relationship that you have with your company, your employees, and even your competition. These can all be highly destructive relationships, and they often are—even if you have not figured it out yet! A tired, overworked, underpaid owner can recover with the PICE Distancing Cycle.

PICE stands for:
- **P**ersonal Distance Strategy
- **I**ncome Distancing Strategy

- Competition Distancing Strategy
- Employee Distancing Strategy

These four core areas will behave as key performance indicators of the kind of relationships that you have in the business world. Adjusting these often leads to amazing results!

- *Personal Distance Strategy:* Working on your business is different from working in your business, remember? This strategy will systematize how you approach working with your own company.

- *Income Distancing Strategy:* This is how to separate your personal finances from your business finances. They are not the same thing, and even though you may believe it all belongs to you, it certainly does not!

- *Competition Distancing Strategy:* What makes your company outstrip all other companies that offer the same products and services that you do? This strategy helps you make sure that you always have a powerful competitive advantage.

- *Employee Distancing Strategy:* Examining the kind of relationships that you have with your employees is key to running a successful business. If there is dysfunction, it will spread to your bottom line. If there is harmony and collaboration, good things will happen! This strategy is about distancing yourself from your employees.

- *Reporting and Decision Making:* The final step in the PICE Distancing Cycle is reporting and decision making. You will need all reports on yourself, your competition, and your employees to maintain a dynamic, energetic workplace.

Your PICE Distancing Cycle will work to keep your business relationships in the right place so that you and your employees can thrive in a great working environment.

The Personal Distance Strategy

You are the owner of your business, which means that all of the decisions have fallen to you over the years. I have spoken about working on your business and not in or for your business—which is the opposite of what you should be doing. Now I am going to tell you how to stop what have been doing and become the owner you were always meant to be.

- Create a list of traits that you want to aspire to. Include things like "disciplined, friendly, bold, intelligent negotiator, people-person" or any number of other traits you would like to adopt. Over time, if you practice these traits, they will become who you are. That is one of the secrets of success— to practice being who you want to be!

- Host a meeting—gather all of your staff together, and chat to them about your strengths and weaknesses. It sounds hard, but it can be very illuminating, especially if you let them have their say openly and honestly. Take notes!

- Based on the idea of the kind of owner you want to be and the suggestions you received from your team, create an "action" wish-list. Everything from traits, qualities, weaknesses to overcome, and more must be written on a piece of paper.

- Brief your team about your intended changes, and make sure they hold you to your new decisions. Speak to them about what you should be doing and how you have had it wrong until now. It is not about how hard you work but about how smart you work.

You can also take this opportunity to incentivize your progress. If you are serious about becoming the kind of owner that you want to be, then the people on your payroll must be able to point out when you are breaking your own rules.

If you cannot confide in everyone, then choose one specific

person—your manager—to help you stick to it. It seems easy, but for many, it is the most difficult thing they will ever do. Walking away from a business that relies on you to run it is no piece of cake.

Hand over the reins, and continue to practice being the kind of owner that you want to be. Maintaining personal distance from your business means:

- Not having to be there all the time.
- Not having to deal with ANYTHING your employees can do for you.
- Only focusing on concerns that involve the "big boss"—you!
- Establishing respect by keeping your distance from your employees.

The Income Distancing Strategy

Your income right now may be completely distorted. I have seen it all—from owners bankrupting their businesses because they take all the money, to owners that live on nothing so that the business can survive. Neither is a particularly rewarding scenario.

In your income distancing strategy, you need to figure out what your business is capable of (after it has been systematized), what you should be getting paid, and even what your employees should be paid for their time and effort.

Often when a business does badly, the first person to suffer is the boss, followed by the employees. Not paying employees what they are worth is a quick way to fail in business. Instead, use this strategy to reorganize your core financial responsibilities.

- Sit down with your finances. What can your business afford to pay you right away? What would you like to earn? Build a bridge between the two—and set a timeline. Based on the two figures, how long would it take you to improve business to the point where you can afford to pay yourself what you want to earn?

- Get out there and start talking to competitors. Find out what they pay their staff and why. Measure it against several other businesses that are similar to yours in the area. Then match these numbers with your current salary, your accurate salary, and your "desired" salary.

- Check on the employee salaries to see if you are paying them enough money. Always build incentives into your employee wages so that they feel appreciated in the job that they do. For example, if you plan on paying your grill cook $2,600.00 a month, negotiate a set salary of $2,400.00 so the remaining $200.00 can be used as an incentive wage. Then you can set targets and reward based on performance.

With this income distancing strategy, you are taking your employee needs into account. Everyone needs to be appreciated or corrected if they are not doing a good job. One way to always make this clear is with money. You do not even have to say anything in an "average" month, because cash incentives are only for outstanding work.

- Sort out your business income at the same time. Your business is "another person" that is operating with you; make sure that you give it the income that it deserves. That means if a particular marketing tactic worked well, reinvest in it! If you need another staff member, be able to get one.

The Competition Distancing Strategy

What is your unique sales proposition? I will never forget a story I was told as a child. There are two little girls, each selling ice cream from the same cart in the same road. The one little girl has no customers; the other has them all. Why? The first little girl took all of her ice creams out, and they melted. No one wanted them.

The moral of that story is that often we think of competitive advantages as huge and sparkly and expensive, when really you just have to get the basics right. For that little girl, all she had to do was notice it was a hot day and that her product would spoil.

For your competition distancing strategy, I want you to perform two vital functions. Instead of dreaming about large, fancy competitive differences that no one can afford, take a moment to think about these two things:

- What are you getting wrong that everyone else is getting right, and how can you change your service to be better than all the competitors around you?

- How can you be different from the other competitors in your area? I am not talking about brand identity but differences in products, services, or customer care—anything that your competitors may be doing badly that you can take advantage of.

If you are going to distance yourself from the competition, then you are going to require outside-of-the-box thinking. That means taking your business as it is now and brainstorming ways that it can instantly improve with minor adjustments.

- Introducing products that no one else stocks
- Providing customer service extras that make your business choice number one
- Instituting loyalty programs because no one else has them yet

Once you stop the "wishful thinking," then your eyes will become more accustomed to spotting real opportunities on a weekly basis. You should keep your competition distancing strategy at the back of your mind all day, every day. When you notice a subtle (or major) difference, jot it down.

Bring it up at that month's review meeting. See if anyone else thinks the idea will work. Over the period of a year, if you can spot 12 little things that make your company extra different, and therefore extra special, you will always outstrip your competition.

Compile monthly reports on your competition strategy progress. Do not discount it until you have tried it. Believe me, after a year of minor changes, your company will be so much better off than the other companies in your area. You will rise to the top!

The Employee Distancing Strategy

You are currently surrounded by complex relationships—with yourself, your business, and all the employees that work there. I used to hear the older folks say, "You do not have to like him; you only have to work for him." That is completely the wrong way to think!

If you believe for one second that relationships in your business do not affect your business, then you are wearing large blinkers. This employee distancing strategy is meant to help you track your progress with the employees that work for you.

It will give you a better understanding of the kind of owner that you are as well as help you identify the kind of person that you want working in your business. "Anyone" that will accept the pay is not a kind of person! This strategy will keep you on track.

- Write down each person that works for you, by name. Write down your feelings about each person—your real feelings. Shocking, is it not? Usually you will find that you are somehow instantly employing people that you believe are lazy and incompetent.
- Instantly resolve yourself to matching what your business needs with the right people. That means firing people that

are not working for your success and hiring those that enjoy what they do, those that have great attitudes, and those that are willing to succeed with you. When a business grows, so do the people.

- Examine your relationships with employees and your business finances. Do you pay them early? Do you pay them overtime? Do you lend them money? There should be systems in place that allow for these circumstances, and you should not budge from the rules you have set for yourself.

- The goal with this strategy is to constantly evaluate team dynamics and individuals. Encourage your staff to bring up their feelings about each other in meetings. Iron out small problems, and deal with large ones. No one can work efficiently in an office when there is someone next to them that they hate.

Take this opportunity to outline what you expect of your employees in terms of conduct. Outline what you will tolerate and what is against your business culture. Make sure that each of your employees gets a copy of these conduct codes.

I would also suggest implementing a system of monitoring, even if it is just the front end. This is especially important if you own a shop or franchise; always have cameras, and review them systematically. Your employees could be telling you one thing and doing another. It is best that you all know you are serious and that you are watching.

Reporting and Decision Making

For each of these strategies, there is a process that you need to go through in order to arrive at your very first report. These reports will then be used to help you monitor and align your personal goals and your employee goals with the state of your business.

I know some business owners that ask their employees where they would like to be in two years, and create a strategy for them to get there. It lets the employee know that you are serious about their success and that there is growth opportunity with your brand.

- Weekly personal reports will show you how you behave at work.
- Monthly personal reports will help you see where you need to improve.
- Weekly income reports keep you working towards your goal.
- Monthly income reports show you what works and what does not work.
- Weekly competition reports keep you thinking about opportunities.
- Monthly competition reports show you how small changes make a difference.
- Weekly employee reports inspire your employees to work towards something.
- Monthly employee reports assist with incentives and business growth.

Reports like these perhaps do not have to occur every week if you are a small business owner—but keeping tabs on the relationships that you have in your business is instrumental to its eventual success. Do not think for one second any of these lines of thought will happen on their own; they have to be practiced in order to be realized.

These Monthly Reports Will:

- Keep you informed about office or business relationship dynamics.
- Help you spot talent and nurture it.

- Help you spot destructive individuals and root them out.
- Keep you functioning on a higher level as the owner.
- Help frame your responsibility to the business in terms of human capital.
- Keep you one step ahead of your competition at all times.

When a business has great systems that support great people, it can become virtually unstoppable. It only requires some time, some brainstorming, and the willingness to open new lines of communication. From there, it is a small matter of business culture integration—which is what you are reading this book for!

These reports will help you make the right decisions about hiring new staff, firing, and working through team problems or your own personal stumbling points. No one is perfect, but if you hold yourself to a system, you can get really close.

BLUEPRINT 4: THE OPERATIONS MANAGEMENT CYCLE

"Operations keep the lights on, strategy provides a light at the end of the tunnel, but project management is the train engine that moves the organization forward."

JOY GUMZ

When your business operates flawlessly, you will reap the most rewards—and that should be the goal of every business owner. With an Operations Management Cycle blueprint, you will get a first-hand peek at what it takes to run four of the most demanding types of company.

The TILC Operations Cycle will expose you to what a great service business should run like, what product-centric businesses should operate like, and what franchise and online companies should operate like in an ideal world.

The TILC Operations Cycle (technology, integration, location, capacity)

The TILC Operations Cycle is made up of a set of strategies that focus on technology, integration, location, and capacity for business success. In each scenario, the business has certain limitations and needs that must be met in order for it to excel.

The Strategies Are:

- TILC Service Business Operations Strategy
- TILC Product-Centered Operations Strategy

- TILC Franchise Operations Strategy
- TILC Online Operations Strategy

These four core areas will clue you in on how each specific business type is able to grow and succeed, despite there being millions of other models just like them around the world.

- *TILC Service Business Operations Strategy:* This strategy will tell you what kind of operations you need to have in hand in order for your service business to take off. Service businesses are often the companies where the owner works themselves to death! If this is you, then pay close attention to this strategy.

- *TILC Product-Centered Operations Strategy:* Product businesses are great, but owners always have to worry about stock coming in and going out. The logistics of this operations strategy can be a little more complicated to get right—but it is one model that you cannot afford to get wrong, because it becomes a money drain.

- *TILC Franchise Operations Strategy:* Owning a franchise is often considered a much safer way to do business, yet many, many franchisees fail. In this strategy, you will see how a franchise is meant to operate like in the real world.

- *TILC Online Operations Strategy:* Starting an online business is the easiest and the hardest of all the business models—because quitting is just as easy as starting. To get these business operations right requires technology and help.

- *Reporting and Decision Making:* Getting reports on your operation's status is essential if your business is going to systematize correctly and stay that way.

TILC Service Business Operations Strategy

In a service-based business, operations management is all about transforming process inputs like labor into process outputs like a quality service. The end goal is the level of service that you provide, which is where most service business owners get it wrong.

A hairdressing salon, for example, may have consistent customers, but that does not necessarily mean that everyone loves the results of their service. It depends on several factors, namely technology, integration, location, and capacity.

- *Technology:* In the service industry, there has to be very strict operational goals that are governed and enforced by various software programs. All accounts, admin, finances, and marketing need to be automated and controlled via technology. The equipment in service businesses also needs to be quality, modern, and innovative.

- *Integration:* Understand each person, place, and thing's role in the service business and how it all fits together like a puzzle to form the over level of service provided. Quality service integration requires team work at all times; after all, this is supposed to be the kind of business that produces excellent service results.

- *Location:* Anyone can start a service business anywhere, but it takes a real business leader to realize that some opportunities are better elsewhere. Location affects who your employees will be, how much you will pay them, how effective you will work together, and how easily your customers will find you. Think about it very carefully.

- *Capacity:* All service business models begin small and scale. The problem is that they do not scale often enough or they hit a wall and then do not scale again. If your business is always overbooked, you need to consider a second branch, more employees, or larger premises. In the service niche, you grow with your customers.

Keep in mind that each of these basic operational structures affects the other. All four need to be taken into account when making operational business decisions. For example, if your hair salon is sold out every day, opening another makes sense. Opening it without the same formula (equipment, staff, location) is a risk. What can you do to minimize risk?

A good TILC Business Operations Strategy will have you sitting down to consider these important pillars every month. Ask yourself:

- Is my business still technologically advanced? How can it improve?
- Is my business fully integrated? Where are the problems, and how can I fix them?
- Is my business in the right location? How is it affecting my dream and bottom line?
- Is my business at capacity? If so, how can you fix that; if not, how can you fix that?

TILC Product-Centered Operations Strategy

All products have a limited lifecycle, and when you own a product-centric business, your goal is to fully understand that lifecycle in every way. This means that you have to create an operations strategy that takes your products into account.

- *Technology:* How can technology improve your product sales? Everything from supply, delivery, marketing, presentation, stock control, admin, and finance can be sorted out using the latest technology. You can also leverage online ecommerce for global product sales.
- *Integration:* How do your moving parts fit together to provide an excellent level of service that goes along with your product sales? The suppliers, employees, and customers in

your business need to be happy—all the time. That means creating operations that meet this need.

- *Location:* Products can be delivered anywhere, but delivery costs money. It matters where your products are located and how easy they are to purchase. Can anyone stop by your store? Can they buy your products online? Do you cater to a specific demographic that excludes other customers because of location?

- *Capacity:* When you sell products, getting them in, processing them, and selling them are key to your entire business. That is why you have to make sure that you never run out of stock, experience stock delays, partner with the wrong providers, or are duped into buying stock that will not sell. Capacity refers to how quickly you are able to move products through your store or online marketplace.

For product-centered businesses, you have to do your research. Everything from market size, marketing, pricing, competitive positioning, and customer experience counts towards your sales now and in the future. Your goal is to keep your customers happy by giving them more than other product providers do.

- Get the basic operations right, and test your systems until they are smooth and clean. At this point, you will not experience many complaints about anything. That is how you know you are on the right track.

Products are great to sell because the only thing you really have to focus on is providing seamless aesthetic and customer satisfaction experiences to be successful. Take note of how your real world shop looks, how it feels to shop there, and how the staff make it a pleasant or enjoyable experience.

TILC Franchise Operations Strategy

Franchises are one of the simplest operations to execute because they already come with a set of plans. Your strategy, however, will only begin once you try and fit a successful business model into your own personal context. Just because it is a Starbucks does not mean that it is going to sell good coffee.

- *Technology:* Your franchiser will supply you with what they believe you need. You should look beyond this to see what will actively improve your sales, community reach, and automation. Modern technology in a franchise is essential to its success, so by all means, add more to it, but never do things cheaply.

- *Integration:* How do you integrate an existing business model with your new team of people? With great difficulty! Franchises need to run on incentive-based systems to keep everyone happy. You have to make sure that your staff connects with the head office, just like you do. You are all there to advance and thrive.

- *Location:* For franchisees, this is the most critical aspect of owning a well-known brand. Pick your location carefully, and test what works there. Even McDonalds has different menus for different demographics, countries, and cultures. If the location is not working with a franchise model, it means something is going very wrong.

- *Capacity:* Franchises may take the stress away from finding new customers, but you will lose all of your repeat business if you fail to become the best in your area. That is why capacity still matters here. Once you reach the point where you are too busy, hire more people or expand to somewhere close by.

Your TILC Operations Strategy will be contingent on your ability to rise to the challenges that the franchise has set for you; there are often targets and thresholds to meet from month one. It can be a high pressure job when you are the manager, but you are not the manager—you are the owner.

That means that you will spend most of your time figuring out how to optimize the existing operations strategy and make it even better to win all of the local awards for best franchise. Once you get there, you can buy more franchises and repeat your own success model. It takes experience and the implementation of your own systems, but it is highly possible.

TILC Online Operations Strategy

At first, operations for most online activities can be automated, but there are danger zones for the inexperienced online business owner. Too much automation can force your business to fade into the grey mist that is "automated online businesses."

- *Technology:* Marketing automation is a must, along with a responsive business website or ecommerce store, a blog, and a competent social media campaign. There is also a growing need for content online, so if you plan to stay there, prepare to invest in content creators for your brand. They are the media specialists of today, and they will help you with repeat business.

- *Integration:* Everything is integrated online, except for people. Finding the right team does not have to be something you do from locals in your area. The Internet is international, and using collaboration programs like Basecamp, anyone anywhere can be part of your team. The good news is that often this means cheaper labor costs.

- *Location:* While you do not have to have a real world store to sell online, you still need a brand identity. I would advise you to sink the money you would have used renting a shop to create a really good one. Your website, blog, and social pages will make up your brand identity and become the online destinations for your company. Make them look amazing!

- *Capacity:* Surely the most difficult part of owning an online business is knowing when to expand or when to pull out. That is why I would never advise placing your entire income on one company online. Start three separate brands online, and try to sell or draw income from each to diversify your income streams. When you need to expand, it means a redesign—do it!

Most online operations strategies are based on web programming, design, social media marketing, and content marketing. If you want to work in the online space, then these are areas that you need to capitalize on with all of your skill or business acumen.

- Hire professionals on platforms like Elance, Odesk, and Freelancer to create online assets for you at a reduced cost. Make sure that you apply real world rules to these alliances, partnerships, and collaborations. You will need deadlines, schedules, and accountability built into your processes.

Overall, for an online business, operational efficiency will depend on the size and expertise of the team that you hire. No online business owner can do everything all on their own; it is completely impossible unless you want to spend eight years learning how to do everything!

Reporting and Decision Making

For every operations strategy that you create (and yours will be completely unique), I want you to remember the four pillars I have given you to work with. Reporting on these pillars is key to sustaining a healthy, fully operational business in the future.

- Weekly reports on technology help you understand how your tech is contributing.
- Monthly reports on technology fix problems and institute new, updated technology.
- Weekly reports on integration show you how your business functions as a whole.
- Monthly reports on integration help you find out where you can improve higher level integration.
- Weekly reports on location check the performance data on where you are.
- Monthly reports on location help you understand how location affects your business.
- Weekly reports on capacity let you know how far along in the growth cycle you are.
- Monthly reports on capacity enable you to plan for tracked growth.

When you empower your operational efficiency by consistently checking on these four core competencies, something incredible happens—you eliminate the main reasons why businesses fail to move forward, grow, or succeed.

By managing operations via the TILC method, you ensure that your company is always maximizing the use of technology, functioning holistically in all areas, not suffering in any way due to location incompatibility, and growing when there is a need to grow.

By understanding and reviewing these reports on a consistent basis, you will get to know how your business functions without you, how it functions without people, why it functions in certain locations, and how to scale according to operational indicators.

In other words, these operational reports make you a better business owner. The next time you open a company, you will have a wealth of tracked, analyzed data that you can use to fuel your next business idea.

When you improve your decision making abilities, you can build yourself a business empire—not only focusing on one lowly company but effectively managing and running several for your best financial interests.

- Whichever business model you choose, make sure that your eventual operational strategy factors in these four core competencies. If you fall into the red with any of them, it means something is very wrong with your business.

BLUEPRINT 5: THE PROFITABILITY CYCLE

"A business absolutely devoted to service will have only one worry about profits. They will be embarrassingly large."

HENRY FORD

The fifth blueprint in the MAXOut System Methodology is called the Profitability Cycle. This cycle was created to help you keep a closer eye on the bottom line of your business. I am not only talking about money but positive growth and returns as well.

This can be defined in a number of ways, and they are listed in the PREM Profitability Cycle I will talk about in detail in this chapter. By focusing on this cycle, the hope is that you will know which key performance indicators indicate that you are on the path to success.

The PREM Profitability Cycle

The PREM Profitability Cycle was created from a set of strategies that will help you to better understand which areas of your business indicate that you are on the path to financial and business achievement. If you lag in any of these areas, it is never a good sign.

PREM stands for:
- **P**roduct Life Cycle Strategy
- **R**OI Strategy
- **E**mployee Inventive Strategy
- **M**onthly Growth Strategy

These four key areas will help you understand how you can monitor the over profitability of your business over time. By keeping a close watch on these KPIs, you will be able to manage the systems in your business that promote progression and growth.

- *The Product Life Cycle Strategy:* Whatever your product may be, you need to learn how to work with the life cycle of each sale and how it relates to business success. Timing and smooth business operations are just two areas to consider.

- *The ROI Strategy:* Are you aware what your returns are for every dollar that you spend on a goal? With your ROI strategy, you should get into the habit of measuring returns in all the important areas of your business.

- *The Employee Incentive Strategy:* The only way to keep your employees working towards your success is to incentivize their progress in your company. Employees that are financially motivated like this work harder and smarter for you.

- *The Monthly Growth Strategy:* How can you measure overall monthly growth for your business? You should inch closer, growing a little every calendar month—so that by the end of the year real progress has been made.

- *Reporting and Decision Making*: Reports should be compiled from each of these strategies to keep you informed about your business progress and profitability.

The Product Life Cycle Strategy

The PREM Profitability Cycle begins with your Product Life Cycle Strategy. In every business, there is something that you offer others, and more often than not, it is a product with a limited window for sales. From introduction to growth, maturity, and decline, these are the four phases of your average product life cycle.

- Take a look at the products that you sell (or services). What techniques do you have for preparing for a new product launch and walking that product down its most successful path towards consistent sales?

- During your introduction phase of the strategy, you will focus on heavy marketing and advertising techniques to raise in-store or online awareness about your product. The more information you can put out there, the better.

- The next phase is the growth phase, where there is demand for your product, and you are selling it at a premium price. An introductory product should settle into a highly profitable price tag to be lucrative for you. You will focus on recouping any marketing or development costs in this phase to break even.

- By the time you get to the maturity phase, everyone knows about your product, and you should be consistently earning from it. At this point, operations and system cycles should take over to govern marketing and sales activities.

- Finally, the product will decline as interest for it wanes. At this stage, you can either choose to reboot the product by repackaging or reframing it or move on to your next target product to sell.

Even if you are selling products directly from leading brands, there are always ways to implement strategies online and in your place of business that will leverage the product life cycle. Tests prove that even adding a "new" banner to introductory items in your average grocery store can and does improve long-term sales.

- Every month you should identify the core products or services that you plan to sell and introduce them into a product life cycle strategy to maintain sales.

- The worst thing that can happen to a product or service is for it to remain untouched on your menu or list of services without anyone ever purchasing it. Sales is about finding the target products then positioning them in the right way for sale.

Your PREM Profitability Cycle exists so that you can monitor the progress of new products and services in your business to prevent them from becoming stagnant. The length of each life cycle strategy depends on the product, on demand, and on exclusivity.

The ROI Strategy

Return on investment must be measured in two fundamental ways in order for you to better understand how each of your marketing dollars is being spent to advance your company. This ROI strategy teaches you the difference between tactical and strategic ROI.

- Tactical ROI is measured investment for a specific action or campaign and focuses on the task that you performed.
- Strategic ROI is measured investment from overall approaches, which will keep you connected with the overall financial return for your company.

Measuring both tactical and strategic ROI is essential if you want to stay informed on how each and every process is achieving sales in your business.

- You need to identify your business measures first. Look at the goals that you set and the outcome that you are trying to achieve financially.
- From there, you will identify the business drivers that support these measures so that you move in the right direction. That means pulling in research, stats, experience, and case studies to orientate you in your goal.

- Once you have done this, you will prioritize the business driver impact on your business measures. Estimating the impact of each driver on your business measures will help you determine priority, which is crucial to sales.

- From this point, you will create a set of strategic ROI measures, identifying key measures for each driver so that you can understand how changes to drivers affect changes to business measures. If customer satisfaction is your business driver, for example, a customer satisfaction rating will be your strategic ROI measure.

- Once you understand your overall approach, you can break it down into tactical approaches that support your business drivers. There must be a series of approaches that you test out that will positively affect those drivers. All tactical approaches will have a set of KPIs and targets to measure success.

- Finally, you will measure strategic return on investment that is generated by each tactical approach to ROI. Then you will look at how all of your tactical approaches influenced your overall strategic approach.

After this entire process has been executed and measured, it becomes a matter of optimizing the tactical return on your investment for improvements down the line. Measuring return on investment for each marketing dollar must be done from the perspective of overall business return and then from a tactical vantage point.

- Business measures – business drivers – tactical approaches – tactical measures – tactical costs. This is the process that you move through when you measure ROI.

- Tactical ROI is made up of tactical measures and costs that result from the approaches that you choose to take.

- Strategic ROI is made up of how these tactical approaches affect your business drivers and business measures.

The Employee Incentive Strategy

Your employees will be the driving force behind your systems and your business success. I have said it all along, and I will say it again—investing in human capital is very important if you are going to create a dynamic working environment.

Creating a strategic reward system or employee incentive strategy will help you find, hire, and nurture the best talent possible for your company. You do not have to hire anyone that applies for the job; being selective and being in-demand is where you want to be.

- Sit down and decide how you will reward your employees for outstanding work every week. Create financial benchmarks, and use an escalation scale for when they achieve something really impressive.

- Your goal is to show them that they can always earn more if they are willing to work harder for you. That means hiring them at a decent salary then sweetening the deal with cash or "prize" incentives to make them feel appreciated.

- Running an incentive strategy also helps you weed out the people that are not interested in working towards your success. In the short term, these people are fine as fillers, but you will want to replace them with employees that want to grow along with your business.

Base your rewards on the activity, performance, and behavior of your employees. I would suggest structuring your strategy along these lines:

- Individual incentives for high performance or personal

achievement in the context of their own job description

- Overall achievement for customer service, which is a crucial part of any business that wants to succeed
- Overall business achievement by contributing new ideas, innovations, and systems to the business for the benefit of everyone that works there

These incentives should not be a "given," and they should only be awarded for genuine hard work in these areas. Eventually, you will create a business based on personal and brand performance with a friendly climate of competition among your employees.

This will motivate them to achieve even more, and it gives the truly talented employees in your company room for growth. Nothing frightens away more talented individuals than a stagnant company, where there is little hope for improvement in the future.

You want to be that company that always retains those individuals because your incentive system is structured so well. Do your research and launch this strategy.

The Monthly Growth Strategy

There are literally dozens of ways that you can measure monthly growth in your business, but the main areas that you want to focus on are market penetration, market development, alternative channels, product development, and new products. There are horizontal growth strategies and backward and forward growth strategies.

Imagine your progress each month as moving upwards on a ladder. Any one of these strategies can result in business growth, and they all need to be measured monthly.

- *Market Penetration:* Sell more of your products or services. It is really that simple. If you are moving more product, you are growing in revenue. Figuring out ways to work with market penetration is one way to grow your business consistently.

- *Market Development:* Sell more of your current products to a different market. Expand your business based on location, or use the Internet to sell to people around the world so that you can expand.

- *Alternative Channels:* This particular growth strategy involves using unusual methods, like the Internet, to sell products and services. While it is the most affordable, there are dozens of models within this sect that have to be considered. Online rentals, outright purchases, membership payments—the sky is the limit.

- *Product Development:* Create new products to sell to new markets and your existing customer base. It is the oldest growth model in the world, and yet few small- to medium-sized companies pursue it outside of the technology field. Even a sandwich can be perfected, packaged, and sold in the right brand context.

- *New Products:* Sometimes you have to think outside the box and do something for customers that you want but do not have yet. Opening up entirely new markets can be a hit or a miss, depending on your research. This is a risky growth strategy, but when it pays off, it does so in spectacular fashion.

Once you have decided which of these strategies to pursue, you can work them into a monthly growth strategy by determining and establishing your KPIs and how to measure them. All of that was covered earlier in the book.

- *Forward strategy:* Buying companies that are part of your distribution chain so that you can outpace your competitors

- *Backward strategy:* Buying one of your suppliers to better control your supply chain—and so that you can develop new products quickly and cheaply

- *Horizontal strategy:* Buying competing businesses is another way to guarantee growth by purchasing and integrating their systems and successes into your own company.

Reporting and Decision Making

If you can keep your finger on the pulse of these strategies, you will be able to control your profitability and growth no matter what obstacles you face in the future.

- Weekly reports on product lifecycle show you how your products sell.
- Monthly reports on product lifecycle help you identify and streamline products.
- Weekly reports on ROI let you find out where to invest your money.
- Monthly reports on ROI let you discover the best methods for gaining fast returns.
- Weekly reports on employee incentives help you to motivate each individual consistently.
- Monthly reports on employee incentives help you to see who your leaders are.
- Weekly reports on growth keep your expansion strategy moving forward.
- Monthly reports on growth help you decide on which directions to take for your brand.

As you can see, these reports are designed to help you gain an overall perspective on the profitability of your business from the time you institute these strategies. Setting them all up will be a hard research, implementation, and testing process, but now that you understand where to go and what to look for, the rest is just a matter of figuring it out.

Too many business owners are not willing to go through this "trial and error" period and are unwilling to try new things to keep momentum for their business going. No one wants to work in a stagnant business, where they are nothing but employees and have no emotional attachment at all to what they do every day.

As the business owner, when you look at these reports, you will discover:

- How your products behave over time.
- Trends, changes, and opportunities to improve product sales.
- Where your returns are coming from.
- A strategy that works, when you need it.
- How to nurture people as business assets.
- That their happiness is essential to your growth and success.
- New and different ways of expanding into key areas.

Reports fuel accurate decision making, and most of these reports can be automated or completed with a relatively small amount of KPIs. It is meant to orientate you in the growth and expansion of your company so that you are always aware of the direction that you are heading in. It is so easy for years to go by with no growth—and that is no good!

Have these weekly and monthly reports delivered to your office so that you can function in your role as the business owner that drives growth, success, and new, innovative strategies that will take your business to new heights.

BLUEPRINT 6: THE SYSTEMS PROGRESS CYCLE

"If you are on the wrong road, progress means doing an about-turn and walking back to the right road; and in that case the man who turns back soonest is the most progressive man."

C.S. LEWIS

The final set of strategies is centered on the Systems Progress Cycle and functions to ensure that your business is always pushing the boundaries of what can be done and what is done—in order to find new opportunities in your business.

If there is no progress, in short, there is no growth and no enthusiasm, and your business becomes a two dimensional emotional drain on everyone that works there. In this last blueprint, you will discover how to keep momentum going in your company.

The CRIB Progress Cycle

The CRIB Progress Cycle was created from a set of strategies that were designed to keep you from becoming complacent about your role as a business owner and leader. These strategies will ensure that despite "daily" life, your business keeps leveling up, every month.

CRIB stands for:

- **C**ycle of Innovation Strategy
- **R**esearch and Development Strategy
- **I**dea Adoption Strategy
- **B**usiness Strategic Planning Strategy

These four core areas will act as key indicators as you progress through your average month. They will help you see new opportunities as you set, adjust, and improve your business systems.

- *The Cycle of Innovation Strategy:* How does your business guarantee that it thrives on innovation in every area? This strategy will help you and your teams integrate innovation into your business culture.

- *The Research and Development Strategy:* New products and services are difficult to manage, and most of the time, it is easier to rely on old products that are proven to sell. This strategy helps you unearth those new gems that accelerate business growth.

- *The Idea Adoption Strategy:* Working with a team of people has many benefits, and one of those benefits is multiple minds, multiple ideas. With this idea adoption strategy, your company will be investigating new methods of conducting business all the time, which is great news for your eager customers.

- *The Business Strategic Planning Strategy:* Strategic planning may be boring, but every strategy needs to be tweaked. In this section, you will find out how.

- *Reporting and Decision Making:* Create reports in these areas so that you can monitor business progress and make the right decisions regarding your brand.

The Cycle of Innovation Strategy

It does not matter what field you are in or what kind of business you own. New information is inspiring, and it generates innovation on unprecedented levels. That is why it is essential for you and your team to implement a Cycle of Innovation Strategy in your company.

There are several stages in an innovation cycle, and they are supposed to reset with every new innovation that is identified and passes into a business strategy.

- The first step is education and professional enhancement. You and your employees need to understand that progress means working on being the best, which means knowing as much as you can about your niche. Training, seminars, and workshops are part of the journey.

- The second step is dissemination and personal recognition. Everyone wants to be seen as innovative, and if you can unite this principle with your employee incentive strategy, you may be sitting on an innovation goldmine.

- The third step involves research and technology. Once you have focused on external knowledge and social recognition, it needs to be coupled with real research and solid technological infrastructure to back it up. When an innovation is identified, you need to elaborate on it.

- The next step is to find out if anyone else is using your innovation—in your niche or in the world at large. You may want to consider intellectual property, patents, or trademarks at this stage. Be prepared to invest in good innovations; they can be the driving force behind a progressive brand.

- The fifth step is to find funding and business development time to produce your innovative idea—whether it is a new product, business process, or system. Institute measurable KPIs, and produce reports to keep track of product lifecycles.

- Finally, once the innovation is launched, you will need to collect data on it: feedback, market trends, and how your community responded to it. Then tweak your innovation and decide whether or not it is good enough to become a part of your long-term business growth strategy.

This cycle of innovation can begin at any point, with a simple idea. You should encourage all employees to continually think of new innovative practices, processes, and methods that could be used to improve business success and performance over time.

The Research and Development Strategy

Every large company has a research and development department, specifically because they are the drivers of new innovation and growth for the business. When you institute a new R&D strategy, you commit to furthering your products, services, and sales future.

- Research and development can be used to develop completely new products that have not been tested in the market as yet. If you have cause to believe something may work, developing a product for sale is the most direct way to find out if you are correct.

- Research and development can take existing bestselling products and make them even better, which can improve your brand identity and open up new revenue streams with a market segment you know and understand already.

- Identify short-term and long-term objectives, and apply them to your research and development strategy in order to uncover new opportunities that you can leverage for future growth. This includes R&D on creating sound business systems and strategy in conjunction with the methods presented in this book.

- The cycle of research and development involves four main steps: synthesis and theory; exploration and clarification; design, develop, and test; and finally, implement, study efficacy, and improve. If you can identify new innovations, they should move into the R&D cycle for implementation in the real world.

While you may find it unnecessary to focus too heavily on research and development of new products, services, or processes, think about this. There are some grocery stores that sell the exact same produce as others, yet they do much better than their competition. Why? Because their R&D department figured out what people want before they launched.

Something as simple as a gentle shift in brand identity can affect your entire business. Your R&D team can be made up of existing employees that want to earn extra incentives from you as they work. Once you have reached a certain size, you can employ people to work in your R&D department to keep your strategy going.

- Identify individuals within your business that are willing to research, discover, and test new innovations, products, processes, methods, and services. If you have never done it before, you want that person to ask why.

The Idea Adoption Strategy

Idea adoption is something that you can implement right away that will help you find out who in your business enjoys innovation progress and R&D. This should also be a practice for everyone in your business and should be tied to your employee incentive strategy.

- *Idea generation:* Begin by hosting weekly meetings on idea generation. Ask for fresh ideas, and encourage knowledge sharing between departments.
- *Idea selection:* Identify and select the best ideas from the week, and decide that you will make a concerted effort to execute these ideas the following week.
- *Idea implementation:* Identify who on your team will help you implement these ideas and who will be accountable for measuring the outcomes.

- *Sustaining ideas:* Based on past idea implementation, there should be a system that turns ideas into processes if they work out. This is how you will sustain ideas that are genuinely helpful—by making them a part of your business.
- *Idea diffusion:* Measure how quickly each idea was accepted by your staff, by customers, and by the market at large.

A good Idea Adoption Strategy encourages all of your employees to come up with new ideas on a consistent basis. When great ideas are identified, they are turned into action plans, and the employee that identified the opportunity should be rewarded.

From there, it is incredibly exciting for an employee to see their idea materialize—which improves job satisfaction and sweetens the cash incentive they have already received for the idea. You give them more responsibility and expect more from them while testing their ideas for the benefit of your company. It is a win–win.

Ideas can keep a business moving towards success, even when many of the other processes have broken down or failed. People love fresh ideas and the rewards they get from making these ideas come to life. You should never deprive your employees of the opportunity to prove their worth to you.

- Your Idea Adoption Strategy needs to run concurrently with your innovation and R&D strategies. Each feeds the other in unique ways. Once you have achieved more success, they will all integrate into your R&D department, where innovation and ideas are the job description.

The Business Strategic Planning Strategy

A Business Strategic Planning Strategy is another key instigator of long-term business progress. It must be applied to all other strategies in the various areas we have spoken about in this book. So in many ways, it acts as a formula for the creation of new strategic objectives and will help you move forward with creating business systems.

- *Identify your mission and objectives:* What is your vision, and how does it relate to your current business goals? Take all of your core competencies into account (finance, technology, service, employees) when you start on this path.
- *Environmental scan:* Analyze how your company functions right now; take a look at the industry surrounding your company, and identify common strengths and weaknesses of the idea before plunging ahead.
- *Formulate a strategy:* Based on the internal and external environmental scan or audit, begin to put together a strategy. Address identified opportunities versus strengths and weaknesses and external threats. Develop your competitive advantage.
- *Strategy implementation:* Based on your predefined budget, capacity, process, resources, and motivation, implement your strategy. Decide who is in control of this implementation process and who will determine the success of the strategy.
- Finally, evaluate and control the strategy by monitoring and adjusting it as needed. There are few things more important than this final step, which means defining measurement parameters, target values, and performance; performing these measurement tests; comparing them with benchmarks; and performing changes along a timescale.

Strategic planning is a core competency that should be nurtured in your business leaders but also in the younger members of your business. When people are able to see the strategic needs of a company, they are more likely to come up with ideas that are suitable for the strategic testing and implementation process.

Use your Business Strategic Planning Strategy to keep your

business moving forward by supporting your innovation, idea, and R&D goals.

For every problem there is a potential solution sitting in the mind of someone who works for you. If you cannot figure it out, allow them to! People will surprise you with great ideas if you let them.

Reporting and Decision Making

Owning a successful business is like owning a shark in a tank of water. Even though the tank begins small, the shark has to keep on moving if it has any chance of being impressive enough to deserve a bigger tank. If the shark is stagnant, it dies.

These innovation reports behave as a way to monitor how you are turning new ideas into positive new strategies, products, or services for your company.

- Weekly reports on innovation measure how innovative your business is.
- Monthly reports on innovation show you how innovative ideas affect your bottom line.
- Weekly reports on R&D let you discover new ways to improve your business.
- Monthly reports on R&D nail down which ways work and how to expand on them.
- Weekly reports on idea adoption encourage your employees to be idea farmers.
- Monthly reports on idea adoption show you how new ideas drive business progress.
- Weekly reports on strategic planning help you to support all innovations with quality strategy.
- Monthly reports on strategic planning let you see how your ideas and innovations perform.

It is essential that you as the business owner make a concerted effort in this area. It is one of your most important roles—driving innovation and development in your company. Businesses that leave these strategies out because they are "not important" end up like a dead shark in a very small tank.

These reports will help you discover:

- How positive progress enlightens and pushes your business forward.
- Who in your company has the best ideas.
- Who in your company is best at executing and measuring these ideas.
- How new ideas can cause leaps in revenue.
- How motivation plays a crucial role in business success.
- How ideas and innovation make for happier, more enthusiastic employees.

When you receive these reports on a monthly basis, you will be able to make decisions about your company that you never dreamed possible. You know those risks you always wanted to take but never got around to? They fit neatly into this category.

Often these idea risks can pay off and result in new revenue streams and expansion into new markets. There are always new ideas to test out and try as long as you have a real passion for discovery as the business owner.

COMPANY-
WIDE MAXOUT
ADOPTION

"Winning is not a sometime thing; it's an all time thing. You don't win once in a while, you don't do things right once in a while, you do them right all the time. Winning is habit. Unfortunately, so is losing."

VINCE LOMBARDI

Now that you have worked through the various stages of the MAXOut Systems Methodology, you have probably realized that there is a lot of work to do!

Like any good business system, this will frame the areas that you need to concentrate on but will leave the planning and flexibility up to you. In other words, you need to start being that driving force right now.

Working with the MAXOut Methodology

This framework will allow you to plan your way to great systems in no time. All you have to do is follow the outline I have given you in this book.

The MAXOut Systems Methodology:

System Success Cycles

In this section, you learned what you needed to know about business success in order to realign your goals and move forward to a more systematized method of doing business. From creating measurable actions to implementing automated systems, there are two key blueprints here for you to work on:

- The System Measurement Cycle: Using FLIC Measurement to create business measurement systems
- The System Automation Cycle: Using BOBS Automation Cycle to see which parts of your business can be completely automated

System Involvement Cycles

In this section, you learned about your role as the business owner and how that affects the operation of your business. Your involvement and the involvement of your employees matters to your business on so many levels. There are two key blueprints in this section:

- The System Distancing Cycle: Using PICE Distancing Cycle to understand what you should be focusing on as the leader of your business
- The Operations Management Cycle: Using the TILC Operations Management Cycle to recognize that different businesses have different needs and operational goals

System Money Cycles

In this section, you learned about the importance of money in your company, how to monitor and improve profitability, and why thinking ahead is an essential part of a successful business model. There are two key blueprints that you need to create from these sections:

- The Profitability Cycle: Using the PREM Profitability Cycle to recognize the key performance indicators that denote long-term business growth and financial success.
- The Systems Progress Cycle: Using The CRIB Progress Cycle to maintain the correct levels of motivation, incentive, and progress in your company

Creating Your MAXOut Action Plan

Based on the information I have given you in this book, you will need to create your very own blueprints, elaborate on research, and construct the systems that will keep your business inching closer to global success with every passing day.

Create your business systems around these strategies:

System Success Cycles

The System Measurement Cycle

- FLIC Measurement Cycle
  - Create your Financial Measurement Strategy blueprint
  - Create your Learning and Growth Strategy blueprint
  - Create your Internal Business Measurement blueprint
  - Create your Customer Measurement blueprint
  - Implement a reporting system

The System Automation Cycle

- BOBS Automation Cycle
  - Create your Business Rules Automation blueprint
  - Create your Online Reputation Strategy blueprint
  - Create your Business Process Automation blueprint
  - Create your Silo Re-Engagement Strategy blueprint
  - Implement a reporting system

System Involvement Cycles

The System Distancing Cycle

- PICE Distancing Cycle
  - Create your Personal Distance Strategy blueprint
  - Create your Income Distance Strategy blueprint
  - Create your Competition Distancing Strategy blueprint
  - Create your Employee Distancing Strategy blueprint
  - Implement a reporting system

The Operations Management Cycle

- TILC Operations Management Cycle
  - Create your TILC Service/Product/Franchise/Online Business Operations blueprint
  - Implement a reporting system

System Money Cycles

The Profitability Cycle

- PREM Profitability Cycle
  - Create your Product Lifecycle Strategy blueprint
  - Create your ROI Strategy blueprint
  - Create your Employee Incentive Strategy blueprint
  - Create your Monthly Growth Strategy blueprint
  - Implement a reporting system

The Systems Progress Cycle

- CRIB Progress Cycle
  - Create your Cycle of Innovation Strategy blueprint
  - Create your R&D Strategy blueprint
  - Create your Idea Adoption blueprint
  - Create your Business Strategic Planning blueprint
  - Implement a reporting system

Establishing Your All-the-Time Business

As many business owners come to discover, being at your business all the time is not the same as working on your business all the time. What you want to do with the MAXOut methodology is transform your business into an "all-the-time" success company.

That means your blueprints will need to achieve:

- Complete systematization of all processes in your company. From what you do, to how you do it and why—information must exist on each and every process function.

- Maximum automation of all non-manual processes, including marketing automation, administration, finance systems, stock management, collaboration, and sales systems. Technology is the workhorse that you have been waiting for.

- Systems that take the pressure off your employees, which will leave them with enough energy to contribute to your business. Their success needs to be rewarded, and they need to grow alongside your company.

- Functioning from a distance as the business owner that reads a lot of reports and makes a lot of decisions. You do not have the time to work in your company; there are employees to do that for you.

- New ideas. Until now, no one has been working on your business at all. You are the vision, the enthusiasm, the new ideas, and the guidance that your business has desperately needed.

All the time success means avoiding the basic mistakes. The MAXOut Methodology was designed to help you limit or abolish the mistakes that keep your business from progressing and achieving its maximum potential.

Your potential and the potential of your business are linked. Once you implement these systems, you will find that absolutely everything changes. I have witnessed business owners go from severe debt to incredible prosperity in less than six months because of business systems just like these.

- Rely on systems to maintain the standards of your business.
- Nurture people to run those systems correctly.
- Trust automation to free up time for more important business goals.

- Prove to yourself that with strategic planning, you can succeed.

From Implementation to Transformation

Creating and implementing these systems is not going to be easy. I have no idea what line of business you are in, so the concepts and information I have given you here have been a broad introduction to what is ahead of you.

Now that you have a functional framework, you can work on filling in the gaps. Maintaining all three system cycles will result in a stronger, high-functioning, dynamic business that focuses on the customer and real world insights to find its way in a world full of competition.

Once you have meticulously done the paperwork and devised the systems that will pull your business out of the darkness, you will hit a learning curve. That is perfectly normal. Nothing is ever as simple as it is made out to be. Prepare to make mistakes; it is all part of the fun of correcting bad business habits.

- Your employees need to be on board for the implementation process. They need to understand that this will improve the business and their own careers—which means that they need to be partly responsible for the rollout process.
- The technology and software packages that you choose will be contingent upon your research and on good judgment. The size of your business and the resources that you have to spend on software certainly matter. Implementation may take some time, so give yourself a month to familiarize everyone with the new systems.
- From the moment your systems are implemented you need to hold everyone accountable for their actions. They will need to receive copies of the new business rules and operations

manual along with a brief on how your employee incentive program is going to work.

I am not going to joke around here. This process will be like replacing the business you know with a completely different one, but that is a good thing! You want to go from implementation to transformation in just a few months.

When you use the reporting system to support your decisions, an incredible thing happens—your ideas, processes, and relationships begin to work towards the benefit of your company! What could be more rewarding than seeing your business grow from strength to strength?

Your One-Year Timeline

I am not promising you a business that leaps from zero to conglomerate in three months. That is impossible unless you have a team of Harvard MBA students working on your startup. What I am promising you is the correction of old failing business practices in one year.

Any business owner—regardless of income, resources, or company size—can go from failing to thriving in a year using the MAXOut System Methodology. It is designed to be scalable and can be adapted in a multitude of ways.

You can break up your systems and reporting structures into two to three month increments or more if you want to see how they directly impact business operations. Each cycle is called a cycle because it should never end. Consistency is key to great business practices.

Dedicate 2-3 Months to Work On:

System Success Cycles
- The System Measurement Cycle

- FLIC Measurement Cycle
- The System Automation Cycle
  - BOBS Automation Cycle

Months 4, 5, 6:

System Involvement Cycles

- The System Distancing Cycle
  - PICE Distancing Cycle
- The Operations Management Cycle
  - TILC Operations Management Cycle

Months 7, 8, 9:

System Money Cycles

- The Profitability Cycle
  - PREM Profitability Cycle
- The Systems Progress Cycle
  - CRIB Progress Cycle

These timelines are just suggestions. I have seen entrepreneurs so excited about the systems process that they do it all in one month, so it is entirely possible. You will find that after you have consumed this information, going to work every day and struggling becomes pointless, and you are driven towards these changes.

The Stable, Profitable Business Mantra

A good business, in my opinion, can be defined by two main things: stability and profit. Both of these are what govern how people view your business and whether they will work for your business or become fans of your business.

- *Stability:* Most companies are not stable. They struggle with inconsistency, missed deadlines, poor service, bad products, and lazy employees. A great company is the opposite of this. They are consistently reliable, their service is on time and excellent, they produce incredible products, and their staff are energized and friendly.

- *Profitable:* Most small- to medium-sized companies are not profitable. The finances are inextricably mixed with the personal finances of the owner. Employees are not paid well, and there are irregular payment dates. There is no money for expansion or improvement. A profitable company has enough cash flow to pay everyone on time and still expand into new areas.

Your new business mantra must be "stability and profit." It sounds mundane, I know, but the bottom line is that business owners very rarely plan to have rock star Fortune 500 companies. If you set your goals too high, you could cripple yourself with how hard the daily slog really is—and that is not helpful.

Instead, realize that building businesses is about intelligence, governance, and pushing a business model into stability and profit. Start enough businesses based on this premise and you could end up owning dozens of well-rounded companies that are part of the community and create abundance for everyone in your life.

Once you have achieved stability and profit, then you can think about expanding to the point where you own a Fortune 500 company one day!

CONCLUSION

The MAXOut Systems Methodology was designed to help business owners, executives, and COOs discover why their companies are ailing in this modern economy. It also provides the solutions or framework on how they can go about fixing these major problems.

When you take a closer look at all successful business models, you begin to see just how prolific systematization has become in the age of technological innovation. Now you can use technology to govern the systems that will turn your business around.

You are also perfectly poised to systematize and measure the actions of your employees, across multiple departments, holistically and efficiently. This is all possible now that business operations have integrated with technology.

I hope that the MAXOut Methodology provides you with the answers that you have been searching for. You do not have to spend another day working yourself to death because your business cannot seem to get off the ground. Instead of working hard, try working smart. These systems will help you get there.

Using the incredible reliability of modern reporting systems, you will excel as the leader of your business and redefine your role in the company.

It takes just one decision to move forward. Are you ready to say yes to systems?

To business success!

Zenovia Andrews

REFERENCES

Chapter 1

Quotes About Systems, Goodreads, http://www.goodreads.com/quotes/tag/systems

Cohen, Jason, *How To Work On Your Business, Not In It,* http://smallbiztrends.com/2009/10/how-to-work-on-business-not-in-it.html

Silverstein, Ray, *Work On Not In Your Business,* http://www.entrepreneur.com/article/205742

Stengel, Geri, *Growing Means Learning to Work On Your Business Not In It,* http://www.forbes.com/sites/geristengel/2012/06/06/growing-means-learning-to-work-on-your-business-not-in-it/

Water Foundation, *Habits Of A Systems Thinker,* http://watersfoundation.org/systems-thinking/habits-of-a-systems-thinker/

Rouse, Margaret, *Systems Thinking,* http://searchcio.techtarget.com/definition/systems-thinking

Lavinsky, Dave, *6 Key Benefits Of Building Systems,* http://www.growthink.com/content/6-key-benefits-building-systems

Sutevski, Dragan, *Business Systems – 7 Benefits,* http://www.entrepreneurshipinabox.com/1062/business-systems-7-benefits/

System, http://www.businessdictionary.com/definition/system.html

Rouse, Margaret, *System,* http://searchwinit.techtarget.com/definition/system

Gilkey, Charlie, *What's The Difference Between A System And A Process,* http://www.productiveflourishing.com/whats-the-difference-between-a-system-and-a-process/

Chapter 2

Baron, Bo, *The 5 Reasons To Systematize Your CRE Business,* http://blog.thebrokerlist.com/the-5-reasons-to-systematize-your-cre-business/

Jackson, Alan, *Business Blueprinting – The Key To Achieving World-Class Performance,* http://bureau4betterbusiness.wordpress.com/category/systematization/

Lavinsky, Dave, *6 Key Benefits Of Building Systems,* http://www.growthink.com/content/6-key-benefits-building-systems

The Importance Of Business Systems, http://businesssystemssecrets.com/41/the-importance-of-business-systems/

Mayzler, Alexandra, How To Create Systems That Enable Business Growth, http://www.forbes.com/sites/yec/2011/11/15/how-to-create-systems-that-enable-business-growth/

Fredrickson, Fabienne, *How To Create Systems In Your Business,* http://www.clientattraction.com/2012/07/how-to-create-systems-in-your-business.php

Chapter 3

Bertels, Thomas. *Deploying A Measurement System: What Does It Take?* http://www.isixsigma.com/methodology/metrics/deploying-measurement-system-what-does-it-take/

Tupa, Jiri, *Process Performance Measurement As Part Of Business Process Management in Manufacturing Area,* http://www.intechopen.com/books/process-management/process-performance-measurement-as-part-of-business-process-management-in-manufacturing-area

Performance Measurement Process, http://www.orau.gov/pbm/handbook/1-1.pdf

Measuring Process Performance, http://www.performancedesignlab.com/wp-content/uploads/2010/06/thepdlab-article-measuring-process-performance-.pdf

Traylor, Polly, *10 Best Practices For Business Process Measurement,* http://www.techrepublic.com/blog/10-things/10-best-practices-for-business-process-measurement/

Using Benchmarking To Achieve Improved Process Performance, http:// www.orau.gov/pbm/presentation/kendall.pdf

Capko, Judy, *5 Steps To A Performance Evaluation System,* http://www. aafp.org/fpm/2003/0300/p43.html

How To Develop A Performance Management System, http://www. wikihow.com/Develop-a-Performance-Management-System

A Framework For Measuring Business Processes Based On GQM, http:// citeseerx.ist.psu.edu/viewdoc/download?doi=10.1.1.98.2118&rep=re p1&type=pdf

Bruckner, Jeffrey, *Capturing Value From Business Process Improvement,* http://www.baselinemag.com/c/a/Infrastructure/Capturing-Value-From-Business-Process-Improvement-352715/

Poulin, Michael, *The Value Of Business Process*

Documentation, http://www.ebizq.net/blogs/service_ oriented/2012/12/how_much_we_save_on_minimising_business_ process_documentation.php

Improving Business Processes, http://www.mindtools.com/pages/article/ improving-business-processes.htm

10 Tips For Deploying An Effective Measurement System, http://www. teleiosconsultants.com/news/10-tips-for-deploying-an-effective-measurement-system/

Chapter 4

Automation Quotes, http://www.brainyquote.com/quotes/keywords/ automation.html

FireFly Point Of Sale, http://www.granburyrs.com/products/sales-builder-01/

Luo, Chris, *How Loyalty Automation Will Drive Small Business Sales In 2013,* http://blog.fivestars.com/how-loyalty-automation-will-drive-small-business-sales-in-2013/

Williamson, Matt, *Customers' Mindset – Aligning For Retention Automation And Loyalty,* http://www.windsorcircle.com/blog/the-keep-your-customers-mindset-aligning-for-retention-automation-and-loyalty

Email Marketing Automation Encourages Customer Loyalty, http://www.predictiveresponse.com/email-marketing-customer-loyalty/

The Onecommand Customer Marketing & Loyalty Automation Platform, http://www.onecommand.com/what-we-do/the-onecommand-customer-marketing-loyalty-automation-platform-

Schrage. Michael, *Why You Should Automate Parts Of Your Job To Save It,* http://blogs.hbr.org/2011/08/why-you-should-automate-parts/

Hardeman, Chris, *10 Ways Sales Benefits From Marketing Automation,* http://www.demandgenreport.com/industry-topics/demanding-views/2305-10-ways-sales-benefits-from-marketing-automation.html#.UpwUocSno2s

Pinto, Jim, Business Growth Barriers & Plateaus For Automation Suppliers, http://www.jimpinto.com/writings/growthbarriers.html

Pinto, Jim, *Price/Margin/Volume Mindset Inhibits Growth,* http://www.automation.com/library/articles-white-papers/articles-by-jim-pinto/pricemarginvolume-mindset-inhibits-growth

Kinderganm Ashley, Automation: A Trend That's Sticking, http://www.thefinancialist.com/automation-a-trend-thats-sticking/

Chapter 5

Stengel, Geri, *Growing Means Learning To Work On Your Business Not In It,* http://www.forbes.com/sites/geristengel/2012/06/06/growing-means-learning-to-work-on-your-business-not-in-it/

Rykrsmith, Eva, *Are You a Big Picture Thinker Or Detail-Oriented?* http://quickbase.intuit.com/blog/2011/03/17/are-you-a-big-picture-thinker-or-detail-oriented/

Haupt, Michael, *How To Think Big,* http://michaelhaupt.com/big-picture-thinking/

Jenkins, Jane, *5 Keys To Effective Delegation: How Leaders Assign Responsibility & Authority,* http://www.managingamericans.com/BlogFeed/Management/5-Keys-to-Effective-Delegation-How-Leaders-Assign-Responsibility.htm

5 Keys To Successful Delegation, http://managementsuccesscards.com.au/5-keys-to-successful-delegation/

Oliver, Melinda, *Five Ways To Work On, Not In, Your Business,* http://www.smartcompany.com.au/leadership/33798-five-ways-to-work-on--not-in--your-business.html

Silverstein, Ray, *Work On—Not In—Your Business,* http://www.entrepreneur.com/article/205742

Lowery, Tom, *How To Work ON Your Business—Not Just In It,* http://www.huffingtonpost.com/tom-lowery/how-to-work-on-your-busin_b_4300008.html

Goltz, Jay, *A Plan For Working On (Not In) Your Business,* http://boss.blogs.nytimes.com/2011/04/21/a-plan-for-working-on-not-in-the-business/?_r=0

Davidson, Michelle, *Work On Your Business, Not Just In Your Business,* http://www.raintoday.com/blog/work-on-your-business-not-just-in-your-business/

Parekh, Jinesh, *Work On Your Business Not In Your Business,* http://tech.co/work-on-your-business-not-in-your-business-2013-03

Hess, Michael, *Delegate Your Work, Not Your Business,* http://www.cbsnews.com/news/delegate-your-work-not-your-business/

Chapter 6

Lacocca, Lee, *In The End, All Business Operations Can Be ReducedTo Three Words: People, Product and Profits,* http://www.brainyquote.com/quotes/quotes/l/leeiacocca164296.html

Measure Performance And Set Targets, http://www.infoentrepreneurs.org/en/guides/measure-performance-and-set-targets/

How To Set Business Targets: Plan To Achieve, http://www.smarta.com/advice/business-planning/business-plans/how-to-set-business-targets-plan-to-achieve-more-in-2010/

Stafford, Patrick, *What Do I Do If I'm Not Hitting My Targets?* http://www.startupsmart.com.au/sales-and-marketing/what-do-i-do-if-im-not-hitting-my-targets/20100831271.html

Operations Management Tools, https://www.boundless.com/management/organizational-theory/modern-thinking/operations-management-tools/

ITOM (IT Operations Management) Software, http://www.gartner.com/it-glossary/itom-it-operations-management-software

VCenter Operations Management Suite, http://www.vmware.com/products/vcenter-operations-management/

Wright, Vicki, *How To Use Operations Management Tools In Business,* http://smallbusiness.chron.com/use-operations-management-tools-business-44624.html

Operations Management, http://www.albridge.com/capabilities/operations_management.html

How To Create An Operations Manual For Your Business, http://www.thesmallbusinessplaybook.com/how-to-create-operations-manual-for-business/

12 Ways To A Great Corporate Culture, http://www.inc.com/ss/12-ways-to-a-great-corporate-culture#11

Why Your Business Will Need Legal Advice, http://www.smarta.com/advice/legal/business-law/why-your-business-will-need-legal-advice/

Duggan, Tara, *Operational Objectives Of Talent Management,* http://yourbusiness.azcentral.com/operational-objectives-talent-management-11245.html

Seven Careers In A Lifetime? Think Twice Researchers Say, http://online.wsj.com/news/articles/SB10001424052748704206804575468162805877990

Chapter 7

Deming, Edward, W., *Profit In Business Comes From Repeat Customers, Customers That Boast About Your Project Or Service, And That Bring Friends With Them,* http://www.brainyquote.com/quotes/quotes/w/wedwardsd131224.html

Beesley, Caron, *Managing Small Business Cash Flow – Answers to 10 Commonly Asked Questions,* http://www.sba.gov/community/blogs/managing-small-business-cash-flow-%E2%80%93-answers-10-commonly-asked-questions

Controlling Cash Flow For Business Growth, http://businesscasestudies.

co.uk/cima/controlling-cash-flow-for-business-growth/the-importance-of-cash-flow.html#axzz2oqxTYwYJ

Volker, Mike, *Cash Flow Projections,* http://www.sfu.ca/~mvolker/biz/cashflow.htm

The Golden Rules Of Cash Flow Management, http://www.freshbusinessthinking.com/business_advice.php?AID=8862#.Ur_qJPQW0Ww

Fell, Darren, *6 Golden Rules Of Accurate Cashflow Forecasting,* http://startups.co.uk/6-golden-rules-of-accurate-cashflow-forecasting/

Spaeder, Karen, E., *19 Ways To Grow Your Business,* http://www.entrepreneur.com/article/70660

Cardone, Grant, *5 Ways To Get Out Of Startup Mode And Grow Your Business,* http://www.entrepreneur.com/article/228748

Byrnes, Jonathan, *The Profit Cycle: A Tale Of One Business Turnaround,* http://www.fastcompany.com/1698313/profit-cycle-tale-one-businesss-turnaround

Kydland, Finn, E., *The Role Of Money In A Business Cycle Model,* http://ideas.repec.org/p/fip/fedmem/23.html

Ireland, Peter, N., *Money's Role In The Monetary Business Cycle,* http://www.nber.org/papers/w8115

Chapter 8

Ahead Quotes, http://www.brainyquote.com/quotes/keywords/ahead.html

The 5 Best Ways To Get Feedback From Your Customers, http://blog.kissmetrics.com/best-ways-to-get-feedback/

Potocki, Kenneth, A., Brocato, Richard, C., *A System Of Management For Organizational Improvement,* http://techdigest.jhuapl.edu/td/td1604/Potocki.pdf

Moldovean, Calin, *5 Steps To Improving Your Management System,* http://www.intertek.com/uploadedFiles/Intertek/Divisions/Industrial_Services/Media/PDF/System_Certification/Improving%20Return%20WP%20FINAL.pdf

Gomez, Maria, Fernanda, M., *Online Stores, The Benefits Of Being On The Internet (Part 1)*, http://www.an-entrepreneur.com/strategic-internet/147-online-stores-the-benefits-of-being-on-the-internet-part-1

Campbell, Polly, 5 Brain Exercises To Foster Flexible Thinking, http://life.gaiam.com/article/5-brain-exercises-foster-flexible-thinking

Chapter 9

Dykes, Brent, *31 Essential Quotes On Analytics And Data*, http://www.analyticshero.com/2012/10/25/31-essential-quotes-on-analytics-and-data/

Anthony, Leigh, *Financial Strategies In A Business Plan*, http://smallbusiness.chron.com/financial-strategies-business-plan-5107.html

Financing Workbook 1: Developing A Financing Strategy For Your Company, http://www.marsdd.com/workbooks/financing-workbook-1-developing-a-financing-strategy-for-your-company/

Theju, Paul, *Financial Key Performance Indicators (KPI)*, http://www.slideshare.net/thejupaul/financial-key-performance-indicators

Marr, Bernard, *Measures Of Success – The 5 Financial KPIs Every Manager Needs To Know*, http://www.linkedin.com/today/post/article/20121004204543-64875646-measures-of-success-the-5-financial-kpis-every-manager-needs-to-know

Halasnik, Stephen, *Financial Measurements: The Key To Your Business*, http://www.eonetwork.org/knowledgebase/octane/september2006/Pages/FinancialMeasurementsTheKeytoYourBusiness.aspx

Measurement In Financial Reporting, http://www.icaew.com/en/technical/financial-reporting/information-for-better-markets/ifbm-reports/measurement-in-financial-reporting

Barth, Mary, E, *Measurement In Financial Reporting: The Need For Concepts*, http://www.iaaer.org/publications/files/Barth.Measurement.pdf

Freedman, John, *Tools For Financial Measurement*, http://smallbusiness.chron.com/tools-financial-measurement-50280.html

Analyse Your Finances – Business Finances, http://www.business.gov.au/BusinessTopics/Business-Finances/Manage-your-finances/Pages/Analyse-your-finances.aspx

Professional And Personal Development, http://www.criticalthinking.org/pages/professional-and-personal-development/800

How To Be A Great Business Owner, http://www.smarta.com/advice/business-mentoring-and-skills/skills-and-training/how-to-be-a-great-business-owner/

Chapter 10

Automation Quotes, http://www.brainyquote.com/quotes/keywords/automation.html

Frey, George, *The Essentials Of Implementing A Successful Marketing Automation Strategy,* http://www.emarsys.com/en/blog/blog/the-essentials-of-implementing-a-successful-marketing-automation-strategy-george-frey/

Davey, Neil, *More Than A Lead Engine: How To Make Marketing Automation Strategic,* http://www.mycustomer.com/feature/marketing/more-mere-lead-engine-how-make-marketing-automation-strategic/165874

The 20 Most Popular Marketing Automation Software Solutions, http://www.capterra.com/infographics/top-marketing-automation-software

Pozin, Ilya, *15 Marketing Softwares That Can Boost Your Business.* http://www.forbes.com/sites/ilyapozin/2013/07/28/15-marketing-softwares-that-can-boost-your-business/

Knowledge Builder for Capturing, Maintaining, Deploying Business Rules in eBusiness Systems, http://www.xpertrule.com/tutor/business.htm

Business Rules, http://www.pega.com/business-rules

Floyd, Renee, *What Is Business Process Automation ?* http://www.laserfiche.com/ecmblog/article/what-is-business-process-automation-bpa

Peisl, Roland., Blaese, Elise., Kaczmarek, Joeseph., *Driving Strategic Value With Process Automation,* ftp://public.dhe.ibm.com/software/emea/de/websphere/5542_driving_strategic_value_oct_17-08.pdf

Autonomy Process Automation, http://www.hp.com/hpinfo/newsroom/press_kits/2012/FallBizPrinting/Autonomy_Process_Automation_Datasheet.pdf

Chapter 11

Carlyle, Thomas, *Our Main Business Is Not To See What Lies Dimly At A Distance, But To Do What Lies Clearly At hand,*

http://www.brainyquote.com/quotes/quotes/t/thomascarl110127.html

http://www.startupsmart.com.au/growth/growth-strategy/five-ways-to-work-on-not-in-your-business/2013092010774.html

Paying Yourself: From Startup And Beyond, http://www.entrepreneur.com/article/80024

Turchetti, Carla, *Salary Or Draw? How To Pay Yourself As Business Owner,* http://blog.intuit.com/money/salary-or-draw-how-to-pay-yourself-as-business-owner/

McCord, Paul, *A Simple Way To Distance Yourself From Your Competition,* http://www.allbusiness.com/allbusiness-sales-tips/16701417-1.html

Javitch, David, G, Dr., *5 Steps To Deal With Difficult Employees,* http://www.entrepreneur.com/article/201950

James, Geoffrey, *Annoying Colleagues And How To Manage Them.* http://www.inc.com/ss/geoffrey-james/annoying-colleagues-and-how-to-manage

Andersen, Erika, *9 Ways To Deal With Difficult Employees,* http://www.forbes.com/sites/erikaandersen/2013/11/21/9-ways-to-deal-with-difficult- employees/

Chapter 12

Operations Management Quotes, http://www.searchquotes.com/search/Operations_Management/

Strategic Franchise Planning – Phase 1, http://www.franchisefoundations.com/franchiseplanning.html

Operations Management, http://en.wikipedia.org/wiki/Operations_management

An Introduction To Operations Management, https://www.coursera.org/course/operations

Slack, Nigel, Chambers, Stuart, Johnston, Robert, *Welcome To Operations Management,* http://www.pearsoned.co.uk/media/onlinepreview/slack_9780273731603/assets/pdf/9780273731603_fm.pdf

Tucker, Anita, Associate Professor, *Management Service Operations* http://www.hbs.edu/coursecatalog/2120.html

Hawkes, Harry, Bailey, Curt, Riedl, Patricia, *Service Operations As A Secret Weapon,* http://www.strategy-business.com/article/00072?pg=all

Manufacturing Strategy Linked To Product Life Cycle, http://www.pomsmeetings.org/ConfProceedings/002/POMS_CD/Browse%20This%20CD/PAPERS/002-0302.pdf

Product Lifecycle Management, http://www.tmng.com/business-operations/product-lifecycle-management

Four Types Of Difficult Employees And How To Manage Them, http://www.bayt.com/en/employer-article-13882/

Chapter 13

Profits Quotes, http://www.brainyquote.com/quotes/keywords/profits.html

The Product Lifecycle, http://www.mindtools.com/pages/article/newSTR_80.htm

Manufacturing Life-Cycle Strategies, http://www.idc.com/getdoc.jsp?containerId=IDC_P9972

Product Life Cycle,

http://www.nku.edu/~issues/internet_marketing/newwebpage1.html

Lorette, Kristie, *Product Life Cycle Extension Strategies.* http://smallbusiness.chron.com/product-life-cycle-extension-strategies-3280.html

De Mers, Jayson, *How To Achieve ROI From Your B2B Content Strategy In 60 Days*, http://searchengineland.com/how-to-achieve-roi-from-your-b2b-content-strategy-in-60-days-175028

Ramshaw, Adam, *7 Steps To Measuring The Right Marketing ROI*, http://www.genroe.com/blog/7-steps-to-measuring-the-right-marketing-roi/2593

The Best Ways To Reward Employees, http://www.entrepreneur.com/article/75340

Business Growth Strategies, http://www.bizgrowthstrategies.com/

Planning For Business Growth, http://www.smallbusinessbc.ca/pdf/PlanningforBusiness

GrowthGuide.pdf

Sustainable Growth Rate, http://en.wikipedia.org/wiki/Sustainable_growth_rate

Dahl, Darren, *How To Develop A Business Growth Strategy*, http://www.inc.com/guides/small-business-growth-strategies.html/1

Chapter 14

Quotes About Progress, http://www.goodreads.com/quotes/tag/progress

The Framework For Member Engagement, http://eai.eu/about-us/innovation-cycle

Blank, Steve, *The Lifecycle Of Innovation In Business*, http://www.businessinsider.com/the-life-cycle-of-innovation-in-business-2010-6

Jovanovic, Boyan, Lach, Saul, *Product Innovation And Business Cycle*, http://www.jstor.org/discover/10.2307/2527405?uid=2&uid=4&sid=21103308540153

Geroski, P. A., Machin, S., *Innovation, Profitability And Growth Over The Business Cycle*, http://link.springer.com/article/10.1007%2FBF01384139#page-1

The Innovation Cycle, http://www.business21c.com.au/2009/09/the-innovation-cycle

Research And Development Strategies, http://www.inc.com/tools/research-and-development-strategies.html

Lacoma, Tyler, *The Advantages Of Research & Development Business Strategies,* http://smallbusiness.chron.com/advantages-research-development-business-strategies-21246.html

Research And Development, http://en.wikipedia.org/wiki/Research_and_development

Aileron, *Five Steps To A Strategic Plan,* http://www.forbes.com/sites/aileron/2011/10/25/five-steps-to-a-strategic-plan/

Strategic Planning Steps, http://strategicbusinessplanning.net/strategic_planning_steps.html

Chapter 15

50 Motivational Business Quotes To Help You Succeed, http://www.epreneur.tv/motivational-business-quotes/

Kitces, Michael, *The Role of Profit Margins in Business Stability,* http://www.thinkadvisor.com/2013/06/19/the-role-of-profit-margins-in-business-stability

The Importance of Financial Stability in Business, http://www.onyxinvestments.com/wp/the-importance-of-financial-stability-in-business/small-business/

Reynolds, Siimon, *The Three Vital Ingredients of Business Success,* http://www.forbes.com/sites/siimonreynolds/2012/06/20/the-three-vital-ingrediants-of-business-success/

Brooks, Debra, *10 Ingredients For a Successful Business,* http://www.smithfam.com/news/mar01m.html

ABOUT THE AUTHOR

Zenovia is a highly sought after Speaker, Author, Business Development Strategist and TV/Radio Personality. She is the Founder and CEO of The MaxOut Group, a successful company committed to empowering, and teaching entrepreneurs how to rapidly increase their profits and productivity.

Zenovia is a master in utilizing business systems that help entrepreneurs and companies bring exponential increase to their profitability, productivity and organizational development. In 2011, Zenovia launched her company Rubicon Healthcare Sales Consultants to help business leaders develop a strategy to increase brand awareness and sales. Creating remarkable results for RHSC, within seven months, she increased revenue from $165k to $2million a month!

Zenovia has more than 12 years of extensive and cross-functional expertise in corporate training, performance management, leadership development and sales consulting from several international corporations. To name a few: Pfizer Inc., Novartis Pharmaceuticals, Rubicon Healthcare Consultants and RiverCrossing Pharmacy Labs.

She uses a variety of cutting edge assessments and methodologies, and she customizes her approach depending on the needs of her clients. She also provide business development strategy and implementation for her clients- so they walk away with not only a plan, but ACTION steps!

For more information on Zenovia, visit:
http://www.zenoviaandrews.com/

28651932R00128

Made in the USA
Charleston, SC
16 April 2014